BOB KUYKENDALL

ᵀHE ADDICT

CLOSED CASE FILES OF SPECIAL AGENT MADDISON CADE

First in the Maddison Cade series

Graphic design by Markus Beige

WGA Intellectual Property Registry 1311898
ISBN: 9780615303833
Printed in the United States

Author Bob Kuykendall is available for conference presentations
www.singlesourcespeaker.com

Printed in conjunction with First120 Distribution

Dedicated to the individual who has chosen to overcome the obstacles.

Addiction comes in many forms, and some are even acceptable in our society. To struggle and overcome might make one a better person in the end compared to those who never fight for anything at all.

INTRODUCTION

Special Agent Maddison Cade, a seasoned federal investigator, is facing his career's most challenging case. Street level drugs are being laced with some unknown and highly toxic substances sending drug users to a grotesque and painful death. The killer or killers are sending a message with the bodies.

The investigation leads to a reunion between Cade and an old high school friend, Angelo Esposito. Esposito spent much of the twenty years after high school submerged in a world of drugs, theft and deception. Cade enlists Esposito for help on the streets, but it's just a way to keep an eye on the man. Cade vows to help Esposito rise above the dark and desperate life he has created for himself.

Cade searches for answers to solve the most talked-about criminal case in Alabama's history while Esposito searches for anything remotely resembling a real life. In the end, one man helps the other in a way no one else has and pulls him from his addictions to a better life.

CHAPTER 1

Special Agent Maddison Cade leaned over the young man he so desperately wanted to understand and looked directly into his eyes. "Tell me something pal, anything," he whispered. "What's your name, brother?" Cade paused for several seconds, his eyes locked on the blank stare of the man in front of him. "Hey dude, we're on the same team here, trying to find a killer. Come on, give me something." He reached out and touched the man on his forehead with his index finger, trying to emphasize the importance of what he was saying. Although touching a suspect or interviewee was off limits, he knew this man did not have a lawyer. "Tell me who did this" Cade said, inches away from the man's face.

Cade stood up straight at the commotion barely fifteen feet away. "Get outta there!" a police officer yelled in the direction of Cade's black Suburban. The SUV had become a target of the local news reporters as they jockeyed for the best spot to film anything that would interest viewers of the ten o'clock news. They couldn't film the entire scene from their position, so they settled on Cade and his vehicle instead. A throng of reporters were trying to get close to the crime scene, but after a glare from Cade, uniformed officers quickly pushed them back. Cade knew that there would be yet another story about another death in a case that was beginning to reach the national news.

Returning to the blank stare of the latest victim, Cade crouched to one knee and gently closed the eyelids over the victim's hazel eyes. As he stood and slowly backed away from the dead man, he observed that the man was closely shaven. The victim's grooming suggested that he had someone to clean up for, perhaps a family, or girlfriend. Cade hoped this might lead to an interviewee, and some identifiable piece of the puzzle might fall into place in this ongoing investigation that as of yet, had no leads. The young man's clothing, now soaked in blood, appeared to have been in fair condition. It was an outfit that one might wear to a low-paying job. This was another good sign, Cade noted. The amount of blood was surprising, and oddly, it was still seeping from the man's body. The pool of red, spreading across the sidewalk, quickly surrounded Cade's shoes. He slowly began backing away from the body, but his shoes stuck to the oozing liquid. The thick blood seemed to come alive as it saturated the cuffs of his pants. He looked for support, but all the local police and onlookers had vanished.

Cade sprang up in bed just like all television actors do when coming out of a nightmare. It took a full five seconds of focusing on objects in the bedroom for his brain to boot up for the day. The last item of familiarity was Georgia, his French Mastiff, who sat silently at the foot of the bed. Her giant head, slightly tilted to one side, came into focus. She looked as though she was trying to understand his strange behavior. After eye contact was made, she stood, stretched and slumbered to his side. He hung his legs off the bed and she put her head on his lap for a few moments of petting. She somehow seemed to understand that he had once again brought the dead home with him and they had invaded his dreams.

He fell back to the bed for just a few moments, hoping to find some energy. Georgia returned to the air vent. Cade stared at the ceiling fan trying to clear his head. Rolling his head to one side, his thoughts shifted from the grime of downtown to the selflessness of his wife. Her light brown hair covered her face. He gently brushed it across her eyes which remained closed. She was exhausted most days with good reason. He thought only briefly about waking her to finish the conversation they didn't finish the night before. After all, it was the same conversation they'd had and not finished at least a hundred times before.

His eyes returned to the ceiling while his hand

combed through her hair. He made a decision to postpone the remaining pile of forms and documents regarding yesterday's victim until he could return to the scene and work the details out in his mind. Sleep had eluded him yet again, and he was showered and dressed before the loud buzz of the alarm clock sounded. He cancelled the alarm, grabbed his gun, badge and keys, and headed out into the thick morning air.

Maddison Cade was a Special Agent with Homeland Security. His small but far-reaching and elite division of the Department of Homeland Security was a government creation, formed within one month of the September 11, 2001 terrorist attacks, with the intention of closing the gaping holes in communication between local, state and federal agencies. Agents of *The Division*, as it was called by those on the inside, had broad authority to access both federal and state databases and information systems immediately after any case was labeled as a terrorism matter. The position came equipped with a certain amount of mystery because so many of the agents' and agency's reports weren't public. Division agents also faced a fair amount of jealousy from some officers and agents who found themselves in the path of a Division agent's needs, because The Division generally got what it needed, one way or another.

Agent Cade's success had come partially from his ability to neutralize these feelings and to create a real *kumbaya* type of atmosphere. Successful and highly thought of in the law enforcement community, Cade maintained a demeanor and a record of service that invited approval. He pushed the envelope just enough to be respected by colleagues, but not so much to be seen as a loose cannon by management. He was forty-one years old, but refused to see himself aging. He was conscientious about his appearance, and his brown hair naturally had that messy look that was often seen on younger men. He was usually dressed in the hip or trendy jeans of the moment. Today he was wearing Lucky brand jeans, paired with a simple Polo shirt and Timberlands.

He was a people pleaser, friendly with everyone, and he fit into most any situation. In moments of deep reflection, he tried not to dwell on the fact that his attempt to be liked by everybody most likely was the reason he had very few, if any, very close friends.

Optimistic to a fault, Cade really believed that most everything would work itself out, and that caused him the occasional disappointment, but his outlook on life remained the same. His people skills used during an investigation were legendary. He was like a chameleon, jumping from one situation to the next, changing appearance and style with each. Working this case, he was going to have to use every bit of leverage, available resource and observational skill that he had acquired during his fifteen years as a federal agent.

Parking in front of the window tinting company that was located just a few miles from the most recent crime scene, he got out of his Suburban and looked around.

Although the hours listed on the tinting company's door, scribbled on a piece of poster board, stated that they opened for business at eight o'clock, the place was still locked and quiet. The heat shimmered off the asphalt of Highway 78 and 16th Street, and the Alabama air was thick and heavy. Sweat had already started to form on his forehead. He leaned against the back bumper of his SUV and started to go over the details of the previous day in his mind.

At 8:22 a.m., the young owner of the window tinting company casually pulled into the parking lot. The man looked as if he was wearing yesterday's clothes, and with grease and dirt under his fingernails, he unlocked the front door and turned to address his only customer.

"Tint job today?" he asked.

"Nah, I just crawled out of bed to see if I could catch the sunrise from this side of town," Cade answered sarcastically. He had the ability to convey a sarcastic wit, while his body language and facial expression kept it friendly, if not even enjoyable for the recipient of the sarcasm.

"Let me guess, you want limo tint, like all the other smart aleck cops," the younger man stated. Cade just nodded to confirm the dark tint selection. Within five minutes, the film was being applied to his windows and he was back in the parking lot, re-playing the events surrounding yesterday's murder and its connection to the five previous murders. He did this while spitting sunflower seed shells on the weed-infested sidewalk. As he chewed the seeds, his brain pursued hundreds of *what if* scenarios.

A bead of sweat trickled down his face, reminding him of the oncoming heat. He decided to walk across the street to the Kangaroo truck stop for a bit of free air conditioning and a brief change of pace. The Kangaroo's huge parking lot was full of customers and several others who seemed to be just hanging out. Several panhandlers were asking customers for handouts or spare change. It was a known gathering place for a handful of drug dealers and prostitutes.

Cade expected a certain number of these individuals at any given corner in this part of town, but was not accustomed to seeing them conducting their business at this early hour. The vast majority of Kangaroo visitors, legitimate customers and otherwise, were African American, the ethnic group that comprised a large majority of the surrounding residential area. The scene momentarily distracted Cade.

Growing up in the "Deep South" during the seventies, Cade had been surrounded by people with all sorts of prejudices. The actions and attitudes he experienced didn't make him feel prejudiced during his childhood, but as a child he was largely ignorant regarding various groups of people. As an adult, he didn't feel like he was racially prejudiced, or had any prejudice against anyone. In fact, his upbringing had made him more open and accepting as he got older. His past had created though, a feeling of obligation to correct the stereotyped image of the racially biased white Southerner. Surely people would recognize that a man working so hard to solve the murders of six dead black men held no preconceived ideas about color or race.

Refocusing his mind on the case, he thought about the toxicology reports. According to the Coroner, the deaths had been the result of a highly complicated mixture of chemical compounds, one of which was presumed to be a type of nerve agent, but the most recent lab update provided no specifics. The toxic powder was being mixed with street drugs, and the victims were paying a violent, fatal price for their drug-filled lifestyle. After the third death, the Coroner reported that the same unknown fatal substance had been present in all three cases. The fourth and fifth victims had the local police scrambling to trace the drugs back to a supplier. To avoid the headache, city council members and police management searched for a way to transfer the case to the feds.

The one fact that had set these deaths apart from most others seen in the Magic City, a strange fact that caused the attention to this case in the first place, was an unusual death investigation detail. The bodies of the dead were all discarded away from their place of death, in public areas. The city and county leaders, in an attempt to cover their collective butts, had stated that someone was trying to send a message by these very public crime scenes. This fact, combined with the identification of the nerve agent, had allowed them to label the case as "suspected terrorist activity."

It was a label Cade thought was used all too often when local officials were flustered by media scrutiny. They quickly cleared the files out of their own offices, and dumped them on Homeland Security. Cade initially thought this was simply a case of a bad batch of drugs and politics mixed together, but part of him knew that six suspicious crime scenes and six young victims weren't all coincidence.

Media outlets were offering many conspiracy theories and rumors for the public to digest and spread around. Homeland Security now had the intense pressure and the task of finding a solid lead in this case, and Cade, as usual in seemingly impossible cases, eagerly accepted the assignment of searching out that lead. He sometimes wondered if he was working fifteen hour days for the humans that were dying, or for the glory attached to any high profile federal case. He wanted to believe that his personal motivations were honorable.

Making his way through the parking lot and grabbing the left side of the double glass door (which he subconsciously assumed had been handled less), Cade walked into the air-conditioned convenience store. Immediately sizing up the other patrons, and not seeing anything out of the ordinary, he walked over to the soft drink dispenser. After filling the largest container available with ice and diet Mountain Dew, he paid for his drink and a backup bag of sunflower seeds at the front counter. A thick bullet-resistant shield blurred the image of the clerk processing the purchase. Exiting the store, he could see that his Suburban was still being tinted, so he slowly strolled across the parking lot, chewing and spitting out the salty shells of the sunflower seeds. They kept his mind off the can of "dip" he didn't purchase and hadn't purchased in nearly six months.

He had picked up the tobacco habit on a recent surveillance gig with the violent crimes unit of the Birmingham Police Department, all of whom seemed to constantly have tobacco of some sort in their mouths. It had kept him awake during the long listening posts, and avoiding swallowing the bitter juice was a distraction for the even more bitter conversation. The suspects targeted by the Violent Crimes Unit were crudely discussing attributes of "merchandise," which were young ladies in their mid to late teens. Any of the investigators would have struggled not to kill the goons selling and trading the girls, should they ever meet in an alley, but they trudged through the case which ended in sixty year sentences for seven of the ring leaders. One died in a questionable suicide before trial, but for some reason, detectives were slow to open a homicide case.

Killing some time before he returned to the tint shop, Cade, rarely intimidated by any circumstance or person, approached a man leaning against a dented and dingy garbage can. The man probably hadn't seen a shower in days, and had given up his razor months ago. The man began to light a fresh cigarette using the one he'd just finished. He was wearing a T-shirt that barely covered his sizable belly. The shirt had a simple stamped word, arching over the man's gut, reading, "Bourbon." Cade wondered if this was an advertisement or a lifestyle statement.

"People dying left and right around here, huh?" Cade asked, as he stepped close enough to the man to smell the mixed odor of sweat and tobacco. The man finished lighting his Marlboro and took a long drag.

"Yep, gets better every day," he said, as he walked away without another word. The dejected investigator continued across the parking lot, toward a trio of shirtless teenagers approaching. He spoke first with only, "S'up" and a nod. One of the teens acknowledged him with a brief glance and a slight nod as they passed, headed to the entrance of the Kangaroo.

The reality that most everyone living in the area knew about the drug-related deaths, and of those, only the drug users seemed to care, weighed heavily on Cade. The deaths had been caused by a toxin, but the toxin was mixed into popular street drugs. A dismissive attitude was prevalent among Birmingham's citizens, government and some law enforcement in cases such as this. If they bought the illegal drugs, and the drugs killed them, it made their death less important and perhaps their own fault. Even though he tried to remain a neutral party in every investigation, focused only on gathering clues, he desperately wanted to solve this case before another life was lost. He again paused to consider if his desire was ultimately rooted in his passion of succeeding on the job.

Shaking out of his internal thoughts, he headed toward his SUV, crossing the busy Highway 78 with a quick wave to a slowing pickup truck. The windows of his SUV were all tinted as black as night, and it actually looked like a fairly decent job. He entered the front of the tinting company, where the young man was filling out a hand-written receipt on a receipt booklet that looked rarely used. He looked up when he finished writing.

"You're ready to roll, brother. Did you arrest anybody over there?" the man asked. Cade was going to dismiss the question, but was still hopeful that he could find someone in this neighborhood to talk.

"Your shop is right in the middle of all the action. You got dopers dying all around you, man. You hear any good rumors?" Cade asked.

"Nope, everybody that touches that crap dies, so there ain't nobody to hear from." After a long pause he added, "So you're workin' the doctor case?"

"What doctor case?" Cade immediately shot back, with a fear that the shop owner was in fact talking about his nightmare case.

"This morning on the news, some guy was interviewed in front of Cooper Green. My kids were yellin' 'bout being out of Appledabs, so I didn't hear all of it, but he said the stuff was cooked up by a doctor." Cade felt his body go stiff, and he tried to hide his irritation at hearing critical facts about his case from the young man.

"Yeah, unfortunately, I'm working that case. You've got my number, so give me a shout if you hear anything. I won't even ask your name if you call." Cade could sense a growing disinterest from the body language of the man, so he moved on to more familiar conversation. "Did you grow up around here?"

"Yeah, over in Brookside."

"Me too, just down the road from you in Adamsville. Look, I know you could care less about a bunch of dead crack-heads, but how about the fact that every news station from here to Houston is pumping video of the 'hood all over the country?"

"So, ain't none of my business." Cade took a deep breath, and tried not to show his irritation at the attitude of the tint shop owner.

"I'm just saying it bothers me that the video has the words Birmingham, Alabama attached to it. Folks are going to think this is what Birmingham is all about," Cade said calmly.

"Honestly, man, if it don't hurt my little business here, I just don't give a crap what people think. So, where did you go to high school?" the shop owner asked, returning to a more neutral topic.

"Right down the road there at West Birmingham."

"West Birmingham? Well, why don't you track down Esposito? Didn't you go to school with him? That cracked out piece of crap probably knows more than I do."

"Esposito?" Cade said, as his puzzled look invited more information.

"Yeah, Esposito, the big all-star from your school. You might be younger. I don't know how old he is 'cause he looks about sixty. But back in the late eighties, Esposito was the quarterback when West Birmingham went to state. The stupid dago got a full ride to some Tennessee college and threw it all away when he got on the pipe."

Cade concealed the fact that he knew Esposito. He had a crystal clear image in his mind of the former football star, wearing the number ten on his bright red West Birmingham home jersey. He could easily picture Esposito in the football huddle barking commands at teammates who were willing and eager to follow his lead. Esposito was the caliber of athlete that every high school coach dreamed about.

"I think I know the Esposito you're talking about," Cade said. "I heard he died after he moved to L-A. Somebody said he was living with some prostitutes and got AIDS."

"Yeah, I heard all that too, and more. I don't know what's real and what's crap, but I know he ain't dead. He lives with his mom behind the CVS in the same house he grew up in. But most weekends he's laid up on a couch at his uncle's, right over there by the machine plant, stoned out of his mind."

The greasy tint man pointed down 16th Street.

For some reason, Cade felt the need to defend an old school friend that he hadn't seen or thought much about in twenty years, but instead, he pushed to end the conversation. He paid the bill with a credit card that didn't match the name he'd given the shop owner. The owner seemed happy for the business, especially so early in the morning, and didn't even inquire about the name on the credit card.

Getting into his Suburban with the new dark interior, Cade started his car and pulled out onto 16th Street, heading toward the machine plant. He pulled up the number for the County Medical Examiner's Office on his cell phone while he drove and kept an eye on his surroundings through the darker than legal tinted windows of his Suburban.

He couldn't think of anyone, other than maybe the coroner, who would have given an interview in front of Cooper Green Hospital. The county coroner was housed in the basement of Cooper Green, so it was a logical place to start trying to find the idiot who had given facts about the case to the media.

"Medical Examiner's Office," a pleasant voice answered.

"Hi, this is Maddison Cade, I'm..."

"Hold on, Agent Cade, I'll pass you right through." Cade inadvertently raised his eyebrows as he heard the tone in the woman's voice which signaled recognition if not familiarity. In all his years on the street, he had only been inside the morgue twice to view autopsies, and had only once met the medical examiner. And until now, there hadn't been a reason to meet with him on this case. He found it hard to believe that anyone, especially the receptionist, would have any memory of him. The woman's actions were most likely connected to the current media debacle.

"Hello Agent, this is Bill Justice." Cade had forgotten the M-E's name was Justice, and he took a second to consider the irony. It sounded more like a name out of a comic book or graphic novel, and didn't fit the man personally.

"Good morning, Doc. I heard that an interview..."

"Yes," Justice interrupted. "I was sure you'd be calling. I sincerely hope that didn't put you in a bad position." Cade struggled to keep up with the flustered speech of the medical examiner.

"I was completely caught off guard this morning when the news was waiting for me outside. I wasn't even fully awake. I had actually arrived early to follow up on a theory, or a hunch to be more specific, that I had yesterday evening about your latest victim. Toxicology sent some very disturbing data and I was planning to call your office today after I finished some follow up comparisons. The news crew being here today was coincidental, and I told them I hadn't even updated the lead investigator, but you know how those vultures are."

"Yeah, sure, so should I come see you in person or just go home and make popcorn for the news at noon? You've told the community that a doctor is killing people." Cade tried to balance between starting a line of communication and showing his frustration regarding the man's media interaction. He realized from the tone in Dr. Justice's explanation that the medical examiner was no competition for the hungry news media.

Cade vaguely remembered Dr. Justice had the look of a mad scientist crossed with a nerdy high school chemistry student. His clothes didn't match, he seemed somewhat socially inept, and he probably spent more time in the morgue than anywhere else. Justice seemed to be the kind of guy who only knew about something if it related to his job. Cade knew that Justice had not purposely sought media attention, and he decided he wouldn't blame the man for the public reaction that was probably about to happen as a result of his interview.

"I knew I had made a mistake as soon as I opened my mouth, and I really am sorry. They were asking if this could possibly be a vigilante, and I replied that vigilantes are not normally medically trained. Actually it's not even what I meant. Of course, they immediately came up with the doctor angle."

"So, go ahead and give me the full exclusive. What did you really mean to say?"

"Not so much medically trained, but trained in chemistry or in chemical compounding. I'd be willing to bet that when you find this guy, you'll find that he has a set of letters behind his name. If it's not MD, it's PhD. If you could just give me one more day, I'd like to get a final report on some additional testing I requested to further explain the initial toxicology reports. I will have everything ready for you tomorrow. Of course, I won't speak to anyone except you. The news crews won't catch me off guard again."

"I'll see you in the morning. Do I need to make an appointment?" Cade asked, thinking he would get one last snide comment in to drive the point home about the confidentiality he needed from Dr. Justice.

"Of course not, Agent. Come any time after nine o'clock."

CHAPTER 2

Cade sat at a stop sign three blocks from the highway. His mental search for the face of a medical examiner he could barely recall was replaced with the face of Angelo Esposito. Esposito looked like the chiseled guy on the cover of every *Men's Health* magazine at the grocery store checkout. He had thick, dark hair, dimples and a wonderfully contagious smile. Sad, really, because he didn't need all the cards stacked in his favor. Cade began rolling again while leaning forward to get a better view of the streets and alleys.

He thought about his youthful ignorance again as he remembered meeting Esposito for the first time in seventh grade. He remembered asking Esposito if he was Italian, pronounced *i-tal-yun*, like any good Southern boy would say it.

As a fourteen year-old, Cade's only association with Italians had been through watching television shows that portrayed most Italians as Mafia members. The Esposito family didn't help the stereotype much because they did sort of look like the cast of the Sopranos walking into West Birmingham's gym at every sporting event. They turned heads at every school function. By his sophomore year, he had gotten to know the Esposito family and another stereotype was corrected.

Cade's thoughts were interrupted when a little shaggy dog darted out in front of his SUV. The dog headed to the call of his owner. He was a long-haired thug standing on the corner as if waiting for somebody. He could have been looking for cops, buyers or maybe some hoodlum friends. Then again, he could have just been in a daze.

Cade looked right in the eyes of the man, sizing him up. He figured the man must be in his mid to late forties, and in need of a job and new clothes. In this part of town, Cade assumed every person to be a threat until proven otherwise. He stared at the man and tried to make eye contact. This was an unspoken statement that he believed conveyed the message *I'm not afraid to make eye contact with you because I'm confident I can handle you should you have any issues with me being in your neighborhood*. The man seemed to look around the slowly moving SUV, and it occurred to Cade that no one could see through the darkened windows.

Cade stared at the man as his heart skipped a beat. He had been searching for a man who matched the image in his head. It had taken several seconds to recognize *this* man. It was in fact number ten, West Birmingham's starting quarterback of twenty years prior, Angelo

Esposito. Cade slid from the front seat and faced Esposito who stood at least three inches taller.

Esposito introduced himself while offering his outstretched hand as if he thought Cade didn't know who he was. Cade wasn't sure if Esposito introduced himself because he knew his life choices had turned him into a different looking person, or if his drug usage had caused him to forget his high school days and all the less popular students with whom he graduated.

Esposito appeared a bit nervous, maybe embarrassed. The little dog was introduced by Esposito as Skip. The dog started sniffing the cuff of Cade's jeans. He had obviously picked up Georgia's scent. Cade almost asked Esposito how he had been but stopped himself. He realized the typical greeting didn't really apply here because the answer was obvious – crappy.

Esposito invited Cade to sit on one of two mismatched and dirty chairs on his uncle's front porch. They had a great view of the nut and bolt plant across the pot hole filled street. Cade chose, instead, to sit on the uncomfortable porch steps. He picked a spot that was only slightly filthy so he wouldn't stain his jeans that were made to look faded and stained in the first place. Esposito glanced down at the gun and badge on Cade's side.

"Wow, Maddy, you did it. You always said you were gonna work for the feds. I'm real proud of you, man." The comment caught Cade off guard. Living in the upper middle class side of town, people usually only made positive comments about others as a way of making themselves look better. Like a neighbor standing in the yard of Cade's half a million dollar home saying Cade's lawn was really looking good these days, while his Zoysia wasn't really catching on as fast. To Cade, the trained listener, this was the same as saying, *your grass looks good, but mine cost much more*.

Cade was a pro at spotting the crap, reading between the lines, and catching all the little innuendos and side comments. It was immediately obvious that Esposito, living in a condition unimaginable to Cade, was truly proud of his old high school friend.

Actually, the two weren't really close friends, but they ran in the same circles. And to be more precise, it was best to say Cade had been on the very outside of Esposito's circle of powerful and popular friends.

Cade's mind churned while he heard bits and pieces of Esposito's comments about past events that had long since faded from his memory. At some point in the recap of the past twenty years, Esposito mentioned living with his mother in the same house Cade had visited on more than one occasion, usually with the anticipation of some sort of mischievousness.

Cade recalled images of a younger and healthier Esposito and the other *Rough Necks*, as they were called by members of West Birmingham's administration. Cade pictured Burroughs, Wesley and Macinaw, three meaty defense linebackers who helped carry Esposito to the state finals in 1985, all sharing their first taste of Mad Dog

20/20 like it was some sort of Native American peace pipe passing ceremony. It was a seemingly innocent youthful experiment that threw James Wesley's mom in a tizzy and landed James in military school, forever altering his life.

When he caught up with the storytelling, Esposito was already halfway through a description of his first date with Jana, his partner in the cutest couple and best-looking yearbook photos. They were the perfect couple. Jana was blonde and petite; Esposito the star quarterback. As Cade pictured Jana at a ballgame, Esposito was already mid-story about their first kiss.

"I really liked her, man. I saw her the other day. She married a doctor. She looked real good. And to think she could have had all this." Esposito opened his arms and smirked, acknowledging the desperate condition of the house and the cigarette covered porch that was cracked and wavy. Cade wondered if Jana was able to look her old boyfriend straight in the eyes when they met.

Esposito's monologue was just background noise for Cade's searching eyes and curious mind which was storing up questions for a later time. Questions that were too numerous to throw out all at once. Questions like, "I thought you were dead, and what in the world happened to you?" were top on the list.

Catching up would have to come later, because Cade was only catching pieces of Esposito's story. "Blah, blah, was hired by America's Hottest Bodies as a dancer and went to L-A, blah, blah." More background noise. Just as Cade's memory would flash scenes of high school girl-chasing or other craziness, his eyes would meet Esposito's, and he would return to reality. The sores on his old friend's narrow and unshaven face marked a life of trouble and pain.

Skip rested on Esposito's leg, and he stroked the puppy without thought. A piece of rope connected Skip to the rusty handrail of the porch. Cade could see the rope was too tight around the puppy's neck. He wondered if the dog's owner felt the same way.

The badly painted front door flew open and Esposito's Uncle Frank yelled at his nephew about lunch. Cade hadn't seen Uncle Frank in years and had thought he might have died. There had always been a certain mystique surrounding Uncle Frank. Angelo called him Frankie sometimes, but none of the kids followed suit. "Frank" was already informal, as his real name was Franko, which only added to the whole Italian persona. And Uncle Frank usually acted and spoke like he could have just walked off the boat from Sicily. He was always colorful and even exciting at times, like at sporting events when he'd have to be warned about his profanity.

It was even rumored that during their senior year of football, Uncle Frank had offered players twenty dollars for taking out an opposing team's player and fifty dollars for a game-ending tackle of their quarterback. Cade wouldn't have had firsthand knowledge of such an offer, because at his size in high school, such an offer wouldn't have been wasted on him.

Through the open door, Cade spotted leftover Kentucky Fried Chicken on a TV tray near an old television surrounded by modest pieces of furniture. It appeared to be a one bedroom home. The light source for the family room may have once been a ceiling fan or decorative light, but was now a single light bulb dangling from a fire hazard tangle of red and black wires.

"Uncle Frank, you remember Maddy Cade from school? He came by to check on us." The phrase *check on us* gave Cade a good feeling. Maybe the string of recently unsolved murders and his inability to satisfy anyone up his agency's chain of command could be replaced by his ability to help a friend fallen on bad times.

"Hi, Maddy," Uncle Frank said in a new soft tone. Cade just nodded. Mr. Esposito returned to his chair and the baseball game on the Classic Channel featuring a game that initially aired years ago. Cade stared at Angelo's uncle through the rickety screen door. He found it hard to look away from the man who had aged so much since the last time he'd seen him. The younger of the two Espositos started talking again as Cade's cell phone buzzed.

"Maddison Cade." Esposito laughed at how official little Maddy now sounded. As Cade listened to the advisory of another dead man found just a few miles from where he sat, he soaked in all his surroundings. Two cars sat in the yard. Seeing the cracks in their flat tires and the weeds growing around their permanent parking spots, he deduced that neither had run in six months.

Behind the cars, as far as he could see, colorful houses stood in need of painting, or perhaps a bulldozer. On the street, several people walked or just stood, loitering. It reminded Cade of a flea market when you stop at someone's booth making all the other vendors a bit jealous. Certainly the black Suburban with police antennas would make them realize it's a cop in the neighborhood, not a buyer. Jealousy should not be an issue.

Esposito listened to a tone in Cade's voice he'd never heard before. Cade flipped the phone closed after telling the caller, "I'm on it," rather than the more customary *goodbye*, and stood to leave. He returned his phone to his back pocket with one hand and reached for his keys with his other. Esposito quickly wrapped up the Jana story he was telling and reached out to hug Cade. With only a slight hesitation, Cade returned the show of friendship.

"Come by any time, Maddy," Esposito said. It sounded more like a plea than an invitation. Cade asked for Esposito's cell phone number and promised to keep in touch. "You just drop by any time. We're kind of short on cell phone funds around here. You still living in Adamsville? I'll go get my toothbrush if you wanna invite me over right now."

Cade paused before answering, trying to find just the right tone that wouldn't sound like he thought he was better than Esposito because he'd moved over the mountain to the neighboring Shelby County. Shelby County, at least for the moment, was not associated with inner-city desperation, gangs, warehouses or dead crack heads. He also realized that while he felt drawn to Esposito at the moment, he liked the separation between things he experienced *on the street* and things that were closer to family and home.

Cade immediately recognized his hypocrisy due to the fact that the men hadn't even finished their conversation about how many, if not most friends from Esposito's past had abandoned him.

"Nah, we live down 280. Listen, I kinda need to get moving on this call, but you're welcome any time, man," Cade said, without offering specifics on his address. "I'll try to get back out this way tomorrow. I actually think you may be able to help me with something," Cade said over one shoulder with one hand already on the steering wheel. He figured Esposito may be offended if he thought the visit was anything more than social. Esposito laughed for the second time at Cade's choice of words.

"Please, man. Come any time. I got a lot to tell you about where I've been and all I've seen. I'm thinking 'bout writin' a book. Gonna be called *The Hustler*." Esposito looked off into the distance like he was searching for his book on an imaginary shelf at a book store. "Maybe I'll put you in a chapter or two if you're good." Esposito moved his hands across the cover of an imaginary book for another visual aid to his long lost friend.

The gravel crunched as the SUV's big tires began to roll away from Uncle Frank's. Esposito put his hand through the open window and gently grabbed Cade's arm.

"Seriously, man, it's great to see you. It helps just seeing somebody from back when I was normal." Cade didn't know how to respond to a man who just admitted he was abnormal, so he looked away from Esposito's desperate face.

"Like I'm in a pit, man, clawing every day just to get out." Cade felt true sadness for his friend. Probably because, in his world, most people didn't show their true emotions and men didn't get too personal. He nodded at the comment and firmly patted his friend's hand as if to say, *Okay, I hear you*.

The SUV rolled away with the air conditioner blasting at full speed. In the rearview mirror, Cade could see Esposito wiping sweat from his face and talking to Skip. He wondered what twenty year-old event Esposito was relaying to his dog.

He glanced at his back seat. It was covered with props for undercover work, case notes, ledgers and files. They were all out of place and against agency policy. Underneath the official paperwork, he could see the edge of a bright yellow notepad which contained the writings for his own book. He had been telling himself for over three years that his book would be a great read.

Cade's writing aspirations took a hit as he realized that perhaps everyone thinks his or her life contains some event or success story that would be of interest to some other person who would be willing to pay for a glimpse inside the author's life.

CHAPTER 3

Cade called in his 10-97 (arrived at scene) less than five miles down Highway 78. He navigated through the police barriers in the SaveMore parking lot of the old Forestdale Square. He remembered driving through the parking lot with his grandmother, Mit, back in the days of the TG&Y Store, when the Square was filled with shoppers, not dead drug users.

Because Cade worked as a special projects agent, he didn't report to any government office. He certainly didn't have anyone monitoring the radio he had unofficially installed in his SUV so he could listen to the local police. He knew he was calling out a 10-97 transmission in vain, but he also knew all the local officers' eyes were glued on him when he approached close enough that he was visible through his front windshield. He knew the action of talking via police radio was what cops did. Real cops, that is, and not federal agents who work alone and have no one to talk with via radio.

Another crime scene meant another reason to try to impress the local police. He would be friendly enough to encourage the responding officers to cooperate. Without local police support, it would be nearly impossible to solve the case.

The case had already reached dinner conversation status and was headed for national news. The local agencies had given up the case lead, but they wanted to stay just close enough to the investigation to get some credit should it somehow end up being solved. Cade thought that theirs was a better fate than his, because his name would be forever attached to this old dog case if the killer or killers remained anonymous.

The SUV was parked within fifteen feet of the bright yellow tarp covering Birmingham's latest dead body. In an instant, Esposito vanished from Cade's mind to be replaced with the image of dead John Doe number seven, which he knew would soon be replaced by an image of John Doe number eight, then nine, if he didn't find some answers. He was growing more and more frustrated because he had such little time to focus on the victims before another one was discovered. He barely had time to identify the victims, much less the killer or killers.

Actually, identifying the dead was as easy as processing their fingerprints. Six out of six of the deceased had rap sheets a mile long. It was one of the only clues that investigators had to go on. The deadly mixture of drugs and poison had only been found in the blood of users who frequent the most dangerous parts of Birmingham's inner city. The suburbs and blue collar communities have their share of drug users, but for some reason, the doctored drugs hadn't made it that far yet. Maybe they were intended to stay in the city. Cade heard the word *doctored* in his mind as he thought about the scene and possible intention of the killer. He had subconsciously jumped on board with the medical examiner, but then begrudgingly decided he would continue to refer to the drugs as being "doctored."

Before focusing on the deceased, Cade scanned the crowd of onlookers. He had the ability to spot a lead even though he didn't know what he was looking for. He knew the typical look of a bystander, a family member and a friend. And through deduction, he could spot someone hanging out to soak in the results of their criminal actions. Nothing out of the ordinary was observed. He made a decision that he wouldn't waste time trying to interview bystanders, as they certainly would offer no help if approached in public.

The lead agent was stepping with purpose now, bordering on attitude, as he approached the crowd and body. A narrow stream of blood slithered out from the plastic tarp for the onlookers to see. As if a tarp covering a body wasn't enough, the sight of blood now caused some spectators to gasp in disbelief, or maybe frustration. Others moaned with frustration and Cade sensed that they may direct their frustration toward him because he was the man who had failed to stop the deaths. Cade heard the voice of the patrolman who had reached him earlier on his cell phone.

"Thrown from a car. It's pretty ugly." The patrolman went on to offer his thoughts on the drop off. Maybe the drug dealers didn't want the bad publicity of a death in their backyard, so they dropped the body away from where he died. Cade acted as though he appreciated the thoughts of the young officer. He swallowed the frustration that this fact was the issue putting the case in his lap to begin with.

A second officer in the distance yelled for an update on the "55." Cade vaguely remembered the police code 10-55d, meaning, *Request Coroner*. For Cade, listening to police slang, codes and call signs was often like listening to Spanish, when a random word or phrase would register.

Through the sea of dark blue polyester uniforms, Cade spotted his friend Warren Lester approaching. Cade and Lester locked in on each other. Cade prepared for some action. Lester had been with the city police department for nearly ten years and had spent six of those years as a detective working child exploitation, narcotics and other violent crimes. He had joined forces with Cade on several cases.

Lester, or *Les,* as he preferred to be called by his friends, and Cade had worked on at least a dozen cases together in the past, and the two worked like a well-oiled machine. They took the good cop/bad cop scenario to new levels. It was the first time Cade had seen his friend since a late-night margarita fest. It had been at Margarita Grill, the best Mexican restaurant in Birmingham, and favorite "debriefing" location for Lester and any other cops he could convince to join him.

Cade seldom requested a kitchen pass from Kelly, his wife now of nearly eighteen years, but on a few occasions, the two investigators socialized over *policía specials* (half price drinks). Somewhere between the fourth and fifth shot of Silver Patron at the last "debriefing," Lester had announced he was going back to patrol to get away from the crazy work hours. He would be leaving Cade as an unofficial part time partner. Cade remembered quietly staring into his margarita glass as Lester explained how the move would get him away from the creepy police stuff and closer to his wife.

Lester's anniversary on the police force was the same date as his wedding anniversary. Because the number of Lester's investigative war stories towered above stories about his wife, Cade wondered if his ten years as a cop had been more enjoyable than his six years as a husband.

"Hey, Maddy, this case forcing you to slum with the locals?" Cade's mind returned from Margarita Grill to the parking lot. Officer Lester looked about as decent in blue polyester as a guy could, due to his dedicated workouts at the Birmingham Police Department's gym. Lester's jab got a snarling stare from Cade, but not the verbal duel he usually happily received. Cade, who spent at least ten hours a day by himself, liked the sarcastic banter, and the quick hit by Lester made him realize he missed his part time partner.

"You run out of sunflower seeds on your side of town? You know all that salt screws with your liver." Cade knew Lester wouldn't give it a rest without a fight, so he shot one over the bow.

"First of all, don't be all flirty with me after dumping me and ending our bro-mance. And the number two item on my list under the category of *why Les is a jerk*: If you would solve this case, I could stay in my high-rise office drinking my lattes and eating gourmet carrot muffins and wouldn't have to settle for crappy gas station coffee."

"Why bother? You feds will take all the credit anyway," Lester said with an exaggerated reaction like he wanted a fight. Any stranger or onlooker to their conversation would have been surprised to learn the two considered each other the closest of friends. And because of Cade's travels and strange work methods, Lester was one of the few men who'd ever gotten inside Cade's walls.

The two friends were interrupted by an officer who couldn't have been over twenty years old. The officer was the first in his family to finish high school. He had immediately joined the police department without even asking about salary. Maybe Cade too once had feelings of contributing to society, justice for all and all that crap, but they were long ago stolen by bureaucrats, red tape, and wheels spinning. Lately, those figurative wheels where spinning over dead bodies.

"Sir, the sixty-three has been preliminarily identified by a witness as Baby Boy, a known drug user and small time distributor. Tattoos indicate his affiliation with the Magic City Mafia."

"Great," Cade replied. "What's your name, man?" He refused to be called Special Agent Cade, sir, or any of the like, and rarely used titles when speaking with another officer or government employee.

"Officer Preston, sir. Reginald Preston. Do you need any of my scene notes?"

"Reginald, I ain't sir, I'm Maddy, or Cade if you want to be formal. Does our sixty-three, which I would like to call *the dead guy*, have any I-D?"

"Sir, sorry, um, Agent Cade, policy requires that the body not be touched by the arriving officers until examined by a medical examiner."

Cade broke eye contact with Officer Preston and flipped open his cell phone hitting number 1 on the speed dial for Veida, his administrative assistant and everyday go-to girl. Because he was supposed to limit his contact with federal buildings and other federal agents, Veida had become his contact, and more often a mediator, with the government sector.

She answered the phone with "Watz up, Mad?" instead of the more formal introduction the general population heard.

"I keep forgettin' to block my number when I call you. That's what's up. Can you use my password and get in the soundtrack database for street names?" He could hear the computer keys slamming away in the background. "I need a lead on a Baby Boy in the Forestdale area. Black male, about..."

"You can't find no white boys to screw with?" Veida interrupted. "Go ahead. Baby Boy who?" she asked. Cade could imagine her grinning. She just loved screwing with him. "Height; weight?" She asked, finally pausing for an answer.

"Well, at the moment, he's about eight inches tall. And since his legs are on 2nd Street and his upper body is on Highway 78, I'd guess..."

Veida had perfected her ability to listen to Cade without really hearing everything he said. She could turn her receptors on and off based on a sense of knowing when he was talking about something important.

"I found a Tyrone Watts and a Derrick Washington. Imagine that, two Baby Boys. They run out of street names in Forestdale?" Cade could see a flurry of activity as the medical examiner arrived. It seemed peculiar to him that the bright yellow tarp pulled over a lump in a shopping center didn't stir the crowd like the sight of the M-E's wagon backing into the old SaveMore parking lot. He watched as the coroner's representative lifted the tarp and bent over the body. The examiner raised the shirt sleeve of the deceased and cocked his head to the side.

"Veida? See if one of those two gentlemen has any ink on his right shoulder." The keyboard started clicking again.

"Yep, both. One has GG RIP and the other has Mom. Aw, I hope it ain't Tyrone."

"Thanks, girl. Check's in the mail." As was typical for Cade, he hung up without a goodbye.

Lester showed up with a handful of sunflower seeds. Cade realized he left his recent purchase on the hood of his car.

"These things are gonna screw up your teeth, too." Cade snatched away the half eaten bag of seeds. "Anything good, or were you telling the old lady you'll be out all night?" Lester was able to get all this out while struggling with the art of sunflower shell spitting.

"Actually, Lester, that wasn't my old lady. It was *your* old lady. I was telling her I couldn't make it for our date tonight. You know, she'd probably like you more if you'd let me teach you how to treat a lady."

Although Cade liked the reputation that he was a loner and maverick following his own crazy methods, he missed the interaction with others. He especially missed Warren Lester because Lester shared his goofy sense of humor. Lester didn't acknowledge the perfectly timed counter punch, but his eyes said *good one* before his expression shifted to a more professional tone.

"Before you tell me about all your fancy fed search tools, Jimmy just rolled up and I-D'd the guy. It ain't Baby Boy, its Pooky, from over by ACIPCO." Cade asked about the man's tattoos. Officer Lester raised his pant leg to expose a muscular calf and Japanese lettering. "See, Maddy, a lot of people have tattoos these days. Not just dopers. Mine means *health*. If you solve this case, I'll get another one on my butt that says *Mad Mad strikes again*."

Any other day, Cade could have spent hours in a comedy standoff. But with dead body number seven and the whole high school reunion thing, he wasn't his typical self and couldn't keep up with the comedy.

"Can you send me all the details? The wife says she'll feed me if I'm home before the street lights come on, and I need to chat with the body snatcher over there."

"You mad 'cause his boss was on the news this morning without you?" Hopefully, Cade thought, it was not a serious question, just another friendly jab. Cade walked toward the medical examiner who was putting the dead man in the back of his wagon. The crowd got even more audible, and two local police officers helped to speed the process. Cade was formulating his opening line as one of the locals nodded at him for the benefit of the medical examiner.

"So you're *the* Agent Cade?" He didn't know how to take the question, so he kept it simple.

"That'd be me."

"Justice called me on the way over. He's trying to pull some juice from one of your last victims but he said to tell you this guy should give him some answers since he thinks he knows what he's looking for now. You coming over to our place tomorrow?"

"I may stay up all night just thinking about it,"

Cade said with a smile. He hid his resentment well. Returning to his SUV, Cade caught the look of Lester and felt a bit of paranoia as he wondered what Lester and the other uniformed officers were discussing.

"He give you any career advice?"

"You're number one, Lester," Cade said, as he held his middle finger close to his chest so only Lester and a few cops could see. Cade returned to his SUV and started to put the scene in his rearview mirror. He hesitated as he saw someone in his rearview moving quickly toward him. It was Officer Preston. He lowered the window and adjusted his air vent as Preston approached.

"Agent Cade, two witnesses who refuse to give their names said the driver was a dark-skinned white male. One witness stated the vehicle was a dark blue Mercedes, the other said it was a fancy, dark green car, like a Cadillac."

"Great, there can't be too many dark Cadillacs in this part of town," Cade shot back before considering Officer Preston wasn't his friend Lester and didn't know how to take the attitude. "Thanks, man." Preston turned with purpose and began to return to the medical examiner's vehicle.

"Regi!" Cade yelled out now with a tone that felt like the two had known each other for years. Officer Preston turned and stopped himself from answering with a *sir*. "What's the tattoo?" Cade asked, as he pointed toward Pooky.

"It's the number 187. I believe it's a prison tattoo representing the LAPD code for murder." He released the officer back to his duties with a nod meant to say, Wow, *you really studied during the academy!*

Cade drove off wondering what led Pooky to his demise. He pictured Esposito and replayed what he had said earlier. "I'm in a pit, man, trying every day just to get out." He wondered if Pooky had been in a pit, too.

CHAPTER 4

Cade stopped for gas at the Chevron just two blocks from the crime scene, which was now a new section of the rapidly growing case file. Cade always liked to visit a gas station or mom-and-pop store near a murder scene as a way to *feel* the community and its inhabitants. He looked into people's eyes, studied the lines on their faces, their hurried walks and their mannerisms.

Unlike fueling up in his neighborhood across town where he usually left the car door open, Cade locked the doors. He instinctively touched the butt of his semi-automatic with his elbow just to make sure it was in place. With gas pouring into his twenty-two gallon capacity tank, he had time to think about the crime scene he was leaving and the case he was digging deeper into. He felt like he was tunneling into this one without a safety line. His mind, active as usual, carried him to a different place.

Esposito's face was acne free and covered with a layer of splotchy peach fuzz and sweat. "I love you guys. I love all you guys no matter what happens here. Let's do it! 66Z split on two, no three. Nobody move, dangit! Maybe I'll pull 'em offsides and we'll have time for one more."

Thirty seconds later, half the fans of West Birmingham were trying to make their way onto the field to shake hands or slap Esposito on the shoulder pads. Still, Esposito made it over to the smallest guy on the team. At barely one hundred and twenty pounds, the number twenty on young Maddy Cade's jersey covered his entire back. The third string tail back and starting defensive corner knew he'd never be allowed on the field at a big high school. He was just filling space on the roster while the real athletes like Esposito and the Rough Necks won football games.

"Let's go to micky-dees, aight?"

"Ok, man. We'll see you there," Cade saw himself answering back while standing by Kelly, the "we" part of "we'll see you there." Cade met Kelly in the tenth grade and instantly fell for her. In a time when only one thing was on a fifteen year-old boy's mind, Esposito was the counselor who told Cade it was ok to stray from the single guy pack and try to go ahead and land future Mrs. Maddison Cade.

"It's not like you're gonna get any other girl in the sack, little man. Might as well go ahead and reel in the good girl we'll all be looking for in a few years."

Crap! Gas spilled over the nozzle as the meter reached $85.00 - a new high. Cade got back in the SUV without mingling, going against his typical routine. He revved the engine and took one final look at his surroundings as he was trained to do. He saw more of the usual suspicious characters. He glanced in the rearview to see his hazel-green eyes begin to gloss over. He shook off the oncoming tears and literally spoke to his reflection.

"Get a grip on yourself, Mad." This mental place was a strange one for Cade. Within the past year, he had seen his share of drug users and dealers. On countless occasions, he kicked a door, arrested the adults hiding inside, and immediately started calling DHR in an effort to get the kids picked up before the lunch crowd at Mr. Sun's Chinese Buffet got too large.

Actually, at around five feet and seven inches, Cade didn't kick too many doors, but he was usually first in line going through the door, and right in the dreaded kill zone. He had to ensure the other agents and officers involved knew he was a team player. He always had to prove himself, make others respect him, or more importantly, like him.

Now, for the first time in a career of working drugs and violent crimes, Cade knew a real person behind the drug addiction. He vowed he wouldn't give up on his old friend until Esposito overcame his addictions.

Cade thought about driving past Uncle Frank's house before heading for home but decided against it. Mostly because he was quickly approaching forty-two, and constant visions of his youth reminded him just how long ago that was.

Cade's mind wandered again, this time even further back in time to the seventh grade classrooms of Bottenfield Junior High. He could see the native-American influenced dark skin of Jessica Haynes. She was out of Cade's league, and he knew it. But while it lasted, the boyfriend/girlfriend status catapulted him inside the junior high school popular clique led by Esposito.

Cade wondered, from time to time, whatever happened to Jessica. Perhaps he thought about her too much, but not for reasons his wife would mind. He struggled with the fact that Jessica broke up with him because she was told he had bragged about getting beyond the kissing they did on that concert choir trip to Dothan.

Cade pictured the incident at the football game when he was told it was over by one of her new boyfriend's cronies. He remembered confronting the rumor mill, Garrett Lawson, in front of about a hundred people, all the while expecting to get bashed by Lawson but figuring his integrity was worth it.

Lawson did not beat him up, but without Jessica, he was instantly shoved out of the *in* crowd and became the favorite guy to hate. It wasn't the breakup or even the subsequent fights and drive-by obscenity yelling that bothered him, but the fact that, after nearly twenty-five years, he had always wanted to tell Jessica he didn't say those things about her. In fact, he prided himself on the fact that he never even discussed the five hour kissing session with anyone.

Looking back now, Cade could see that even though the year or so after the break up was the worst time in his life, the event was a turning point for most future life choices. Years after the junior high break up, Cade had worked for the FBI, had served the country six years in an unusual and classified combination of Army and Naval Intelligence, had walked the halls of Congress in DC, and even visited the White House on more than one occasion.

On his last trip to the White House (actually, it was the Old Executive Office Building, where the real work is done), he stood in the marbled corridor and let Jessica pass through his mind. He wondered if Jessica's husband or any of his potbellied friends had reached the same level of success. As he turned slightly to see his toned reflection (the results of his daily jogging around the DC Mall), he wondered if Jessica's husband or any of those who tormented him back then could run six miles in under an hour.

He vowed to track Jessica down one day just to tell her he never said those things and that he had truly cared for her. He might stress the words *cared for*, so as not to give the impression he was trying to win her back after all these years. After all, had it not been for the breakup with Jessica, he wouldn't have moved from public to private school and met his high school sweetheart, Kelly. She was his best friend, soul mate and the calming force in his hectic life.

Another positive result of the loss of his first love was the concept, *Single Lane Bridge*. He had created this term to use in presentations he made to new agents and new investigator hires around the state. Cade was frequently invited to share his unusual thought process and anecdotal stories with rookie investigators. The feedback from his presentations made him think his *Single Lane Bridge* concept was destined for best seller number two. It was to be unveiled after the release of his best seller number one which was still in the coffee stained tablet under the mess of his backseat.

The six Power Point slides were explained to audiences with great passion as Cade conveyed his *Single Lane Bridge* concept of police work and human interaction. Cade spoke passionately with investigators about the possibility of one single conversation with one victim or subject having a profound impact on the direction of his or her investigation, and perhaps his or her life. He used an analogy of two car drivers facing each other on a single lane bridge. With dramatic hand gestures and body language, he would explain that these two drivers were each on their own path to different places in the world, but for just one brief moment, they must interact with each other before either can advance. The two must deal with each other, if only for a moment, but this brief interaction may alter the other's course.

Cade was an average person and an average investigator, but if he had one gift, it was his speaking ability. He could convey just about any message to just about any group of individuals. The presentations gave him an opportunity to tell total strangers all about his seventh grade love and how she broke his heart, and how he ultimately came out ahead by using the incident to make better life choices. He saw himself on stage as a retired federal agent, speaking to a crowd of hundreds about the topics in one of his yet-to-be completed books. In reality, he knew he'd be fortunate to get booked by "Speed Racer," the producer of a Birmingham morning radio show, Rick and Bubba, but fantasies about calls from Oprah were a frequent occurrence none the less.

Crap! Brakes slammed as Cade's mental roller coaster went from one extreme to the next. He had reached Hwy 280 traffic on the southeast side of Birmingham. The ride home was always jammed because so many people were willing to tolerate the traffic for the *over-the-mountain* lifestyle.

It was just a few minutes after 7:00 p.m. Some neighborhood kids were in the final innings of a wiffleball game on his plush lawn. After parking the government car out of sight, he heard the poolside speakers and knew Kelly and their own kids were out back. The three level home, with its nearly five thousand square feet, gave plenty of room for Cade to make it upstairs to change into a bathing suit and return to mount a surprise cannonball attack.

It was Wednesday night, ladies night for Kelly and her best friends, so she'd be leaving soon for some much deserved getaway time. Because he made it home so late, the girls would most likely only make it for coffee and girly discussion, but still, it was a retreat. Cade had no idea what went on during these ritual outings and was sure he didn't need the details. Whatever took place, Kelly certainly needed a frequent break after eighteen years of marriage to the cannonball king.

"Daddy's home!" Splash.

After judging his kids' best dive and *I'm a pencil* jump, and playing two rounds of Marco Polo, Cade joined his wife, the referee and lifeguard. He ignored the empty lounger and motioned for her to scoot over.

"You're wet, goofball," she said, but offered a kiss as a consolation prize. "I've been chasing our kids all day but heard someone at the grocery store say you think it's a doctor now. So are you getting close?"

"I didn't say it was a doctor, the freakin' coroner said it was a doctor. People all over town are saying I'm chasing some doctor."

"Watch, Daddy!"

"Hold on a second," Cade said, and the look on Kelly's face told him she was more interested in him interacting with the kids than finishing his latest story of the never ending case. He turned to watch his six year-old execute the perfect belly flop in an attempt at a dive. He wondered if Kelly had been working with him, as it occurred to him that this was only the second or third time he'd seen his kids swim all summer.

"I gotta go. The girls are waiting," Kelly said, as she

offered a second kiss. "I'll see you in a bit unless I decide to never come back." Cade grabbed her for a third.

"Gross!" the kids shouted in unison. Cade felt the contrast between being alone in his SUV all day in the filthiest parts of town and being with his family. He wished the latter happened more than the first.

"What do I do for dinner?"

"You're an investigator. Investigate the fridge."

"How about a drink?"

"Look under your seat, Mr. Observant," she yelled over her shoulder as she disappeared inside. He reached underneath his wicker lounge chair and recovered a nearly cold can of beer. He wondered how many nights she had put cold beer under the chair until it turned warm. He also tried to remember if she'd been such a smart aleck herself when they first married. Maybe he was infecting everybody he knew with the sarcastic attitude.

More sarcasm was shared over pizza at the kitchen table without Kelly. Madelyn was first with an offhanded remark about her little brother's handwriting. He had written, *my pisa* on his cardboard napkin.

"Duh, stupid. I'm six and a half," he fired back in Cade family fashion.

With Maddison in charge, the kids got in bed much too late for a school night, and Donavan without even brushing his teeth.

Georgia was the last to get his full attention. She had been patiently waiting through discussions of bath or skip bath; tv on or off; and why sweet tea before bedtime is a bad idea. After grabbing the second and maximum per-day beer from the fridge, Cade sat on the floor with the over-sized dog. She nudged him for quick attention, leaving a line of slobber from his thigh to knee. He rubbed her with his left hand, periodically stopping long enough to take sips from the bottle. She only once pawed his hand in protest, spilling beer that Kelly would certainly later be able to smell on the living room rug.

With his free hand, he wrote a draft of an affidavit for a search warrant to legally review e-mails found within a Dell desktop computer of a man suspected of funneling money to the Middle East. The computer had been stored in an Uncle Bob's storage facility for eight years. The experienced agent was using all his writing skills to convey the probability that evidence existed on the hard drive because the only known facts were that the computer's owner's name was Hussain something-or-other, and the winner of the abandoned storage unit auction already stumbled across documents with "foreign writing" when looking for "lady photos." He fell asleep somewhere between thoughts of Jimmy-John's photo descriptions and his own thoughts of throwing away the computer and claiming the circuits were damaged beyond repair.

Cade jumped out of a deep sleep as Kelly attempted to creep in past the guard dog asleep at his side on the unforgiving living room rug. Papers were spread across and around his outstretched legs. Some had been soaked by his unfinished and overturned beer. Even as he came around, he could tell she must certainly be frustrated by leaving a relaxing evening with girlfriends to return to the mess of a house he seemed to constantly cause for her.

They made it to bed within minutes with little discussion. Georgia was content to stay in the living room mess. After his power nap, Cade could have returned to the report writing, but forced himself to sleep to avoid the possibility of another discussion about how he was ignoring his share of household obligations.

CHAPTER 5

The cell phone vibrated off the nightstand just before 6:00 a.m. Cade rolled out of bed and retrieved the annoyance from underneath the bed. He opened the phone and made it into the closet so he wouldn't wake Kelly and the handsome six year-old sleeping with his feet in her ribs.

"Maddison Cade." He was formal even for six in the morning, but his voice was dry and horse.

"Didn't mean to wake you, Agent Cade."

"I'm up," Cade responded, feeling a need to answer untruthfully.

"It's Officer Preston from the West Precinct." Cade's brain worked at lightning speed all day in a hundred different directions, but he found it hard to launch in the morning. Feeling a bit of rejection, Officer Preston said, "Reginald, from the sixty-three yesterday."

"Oh, sorry, Reginald. Yeah. What's up, man?"

"I just got in and found a report of a caller last night who said he hoped we caught the S-O-B who

Kuykendall | The Addict

killed Pooky."

"That's great, Regi. Can you maybe type that up and send it to me in a strip-o-gram?" Cade said, because he lacked the ability to check his words and curtail his smart mouth so early in the morning.

"Sir, I'm only calling so early because the caller described the car as a big sedan like the people over in Forestdale, but he also said the car had a Pennsylvania license plate. The caller said he used to live in Pennsylvania, so he recognized the coloring. I could have our NCIC operator check our records here to see if we've had any accidents or violations in the area involving a Pennsylvania-registered vehicle."

"That sounds great, man. I'll call you later, when I finish my workout. That's what I was doing when you called."

He made two back-to-back calls. The first was to Veida's voicemail, and the second was to the Birmingham's North Precinct dispatcher. For Veida, he left his typical verbose message about the caller, the Pennsylvania tag and the latest off-color joke she would certainly appreciate. The message for Lester, because he wasn't sure who might be listening when Lester checked in, was simply, "Call Maddy." Maybe between the new Pennsylvania discovery and the highly anticipated information from the Medical Examiner's Office, the day would be a great one.

The second incoming call of the day came just after Cade's record-time shower. Expecting to hear Veida, who was much quicker than Lester, he was surprised to hear a voice which, after several seconds, he recognized as Esposito's. The Caller ID showed the call was being placed from a pay phone somewhere in the 798 prefix. This was the same telephone prefix assigned to most Forestdale telephone lines. The same prefix, no doubt, of the SaveMore where Pooky was last seen.

"Hey, Mad. I just wanted to make sure you really gave me the bat phone number, man."

"Yeah, but don't use it much or the government will run out of money."

"Maddy, I really wanted to call and thank you for coming by yesterday. Nobody has even tried to look for me in years. It's like I went from being on the top of the world to not even existing. It really helps that you talked with me. I'm getting better, man. I'm clean and healthy. I ride my bike everywhere, and I'm really in good shape. Listen, if I can do anything for you man, like any police stuff, I'll do anything." Cade still had problems seeing the old Esposito and the new Esposito as the same person.

Typically very talkative, Cade paused to decide whether to be counselor, mother, parole officer or friend. Esposito was still rambling on with mushy *love you man* talk. "You coming out this way today? I'd love to take a ride in the front seat of a police car. Seriously, Maddy, I'm real close man, real close to slipping this freakin' noose off my neck. I just need to keep busy. Even if you got some yard work or something I can do."

Cade didn't respond, but he immediately realized the gravity of Esposito's words. Esposito, a man voted best looking, best all-around, best of everything in a past life had just asked for the opportunity to clean gutters for a few bucks.

"I just need a purpose, man. I want to do something constructive before I die." Cade allowed the word die to resonate for a moment.

"I'll pick you up at noon for Taco Bell, and we'll talk about it." Cade didn't disclose his reason for being on Esposito's side of town. He didn't really feel guilty that Esposito would think he drove out of his way for a friendly visit. He truly wanted to spend some quality time with Esposito, but the reunion couldn't have come at a worse time with two fresh leads awaiting attention.

He checked the time on his Nextel at least a dozen times before leaving for the dog and pony show with Dr. Justice. He figured Justice would put on a nice production. Cade had decided to start over with Justice and make friends with the man he so desperately needed on his side.

After parking illegally, badging his way through security, and walking through the maze of drab corridors underneath Cooper Green Hospital, Cade pushed open the left side of the double doors leading to the coroner's examining room.

"Right on time there, Agent Cade," the monotone voice said. The sound of a click indicated Justice had turned off the recorder being used to document the autopsy of a young black man. Cade looked at the deceased only long enough to determine it wasn't Pooky. It bothered him that he could not even associate a name or victim number to the dead man who he assumed was one of the first six in his case.

"So all the stainless steel in here is for seeing behind your back and not a cool fashion trend. I should have known." Cade hoped the humor would be a fresh start.

"Actually, I smelled you coming. Which is sad coming from a morgue, don't you think?" Justice said, still focused on his scalpel. With the quick hit of sarcasm, Cade's uncertainty of Justice vanished. He instantly liked the man and relaxed for the conversation. Before the two men could kick off a new and less confrontational relationship, Justice shifted to serious and looked directly at Cade who found it hard to look away from the resting bodies waiting for Justice's review.

"Three of your boys are still here. I know you identified them, but I still call them Cinco, Seis and Siete." Cade took a moment to recall his Spanish and felt comforted that, at least, his victim count matched Justice's. "In case you don't remember, this here is Mr. Cinco," Justice said, as he put his hand on the man's shoulder. Cade tried to look like a cool and relaxed criminal investigator, but he was a little freaked out by the whole scene.

The examiner's voice dropped an octave, and the tone became even more serious. "We ran all the boys with liquid chromatography..." Cade hated to interrupt because he knew he'd sound so unscientific.

"Doc, English."

"Ok, cop talk. This guy was pretty jacked up. He never felt the fall 'cause he was dead long before the somersault. This stuff is scary, man. And what makes it worse for us, and for you, I guess, is that the compounding seems to be changing with every victim. It's hard to narrow down because it's affecting each victim a little differently. This was not cooked up in some crack house. It's the real deal. You really gotta watch your back side on this one."

"So you know what's in it?" Cade asked, even though he figured the answer would involve some formula he wouldn't understand.

"Well, like I said, it seems to be changing with each victim, but I think it's because of a second substance being added to the mix in different proportions each time. Toxicology is still digging, but I think I'm in the ballpark and that's what I wanted to show you."

Cade folded his arms when he heard the phrase "show you." He tried to stop what he knew was an uninviting posture, but his arms had already uncontrollably shifted due to the creepiness level.

"Look at Cinco here," Justice said, as he twisted the dial on the contraption spreading the man's chest cavity. "The marks on this guy's arms say he's a twice-a-day shooter. Track marks everywhere. So we know the stuff cooks well. This guy has blood in his nose, eyes and ears. He also had a fresh lesion on back of his head."

"Wasn't number five thrown from a car?"

"Yes, but the lesion is not from that type of injury. This guy fell in a controlled environment, like a coffee table encounter."

"Most crack houses don't come equipped with coffee tables, but I understand what you're saying."

"This guy was dizzy. The blood around the optics suggests something went haywire up here. He was throwing up and had a major case of bloody diarrhea. All of this points to a ricin case."

"Ricin?"

"Yeah, ricin, but there's more. A straight ricin case means the victim starts struggling to breathe. They might even start to hallucinate. But all this just looks like a crazy trip, you follow? They lay down, or fall, just about the time their heart rate really climbs up there. This pumps the poison through all their organs. If there's enough in their system, they die, usually from respiratory failure."

"So it's always intravenous?"

"No, ricin can be swallowed, injected or even snorted. It's mostly colorless or off white and doesn't have a strong odor. But your victims weren't found in typical cocaine hot spots. You're in crack country where these guys were dropped. Plus, these guys don't have any nasal cavity findings to suggest it was snorted."

"Ok, so do you know how hard ricin is to get?"

"I said it looks like ricin, I didn't say it *is* ricin. And even if it is, it's tricky to nail down because of the other ingredient. This is where it gets a little scary." Justice quickly moved around Cinco, almost at a jog. He pulled back the sheet covering a man he introduced as Sies. "From a scientist's perspective, this is actually pretty cool stuff," Justice said, as he put on a new pair of gloves. "No offense, Number Seven."

Cade slowly walked toward the new show and tell corpse. He felt the same way he did at Margarita Grill when he walked to the bathroom after one too many beers. He felt okay, but knew he could be sick if he thought about it long enough. Justice had a part of the man's stomach in his hands before Cade could reach the gurney-side viewing area. "Look at this guy's gut."

"I don't know what a normal gut is supposed to look like, Doc."

"More fleshy than this."

"Too much fast food?"

"No," Justice continued, looking straight at Cade. "This was cooked." Justice stared at Cade who stared at part of the man's internal organs. Justice spoke slowly to let it sink in. "Picture this. Your victims inject a mixture of ricin and what I believe is pentachlorophenol."

"Penta what?"

"Pentachlorophenol. It's used mostly as a weed killer and commercial grade insecticide. I think it also goes in the mix to make that goo you see on railroad ties and the bottom of utility poles." Cade pictured a series of the telephone poles and liked Justice's patient description.

"So your unlucky victim struggles to breathe. Then comes the vomiting, diarrhea and dizziness. He goes down for the count. Once horizontal, his heart pumps the chemicals to all his organs. The fascinating thing about the drug mixture, cocktail really, is that the victim probably has chills, but the pentachlorophenol makes him warm on the inside. It'd be like sitting in a hot tub in the winter."

"Bathing suit or birthday suit?"

"Remind me not to come over for your next hot tub party," Justice fired back, unwilling to divert from his tutorial. "The poor schmuck feels pretty good, minus the diarrhea, and maybe even euphoric because of the contrasting hot and cold. So he stays down to ride out the trip and basically cooks from the inside out. I'm just not sure if your killer is using the second ingredient to make sure they die, or if he thinks it'll dissolve or hide the ricin."

Cade stared at Seis and Justice let him take all the time he needed.

"Holy crap, this guy *is* a doctor."

"Well, again, I misspoke this morning, and I apologize. I'd actually say the field of suspects is open to doctors, scientists and those trained by the military."

"Tell me again why he can't be a vigilante?"

"Vigilantes are good old boys with knives and sticks. Someone so well educated doesn't live in the crap these boys are coming from." Justice let Cade process the information and compare it with known information.

He seemed reluctant to give too much of his opinion and tried to stick to his scientific findings. "May I offer one thought?"

"Please. As many as you have," Cade sincerely answered.

"I have a bad feeling about this. This guy's not knockin' off dopers to get his rocks off. I think he's practicing." Cade didn't join in Justice's thought process. He looked from Sies to Cinco and back again. Justice didn't know if Cade was following along, or if he was off on a thought process of his own. He waited until Cade's eyes returned, and after a pause for effect, he continued. "Maybe he's practicing for something much bigger."

"Why can't he just be a sick, twisted jerk, even a doctor jerk, killing folks?"

"Because then you'd have a serial killer, and serial killers kill for the attention."

"And you were interviewed on the news yesterday."

"But nobody tuned in. Don't you see, nobody cares about these guys because they're users to begin with. These guys are the scum of the earth. You could kill anybody with this mixture..."

"We're not all doin' drugs every day, Doc."

"That's just it, Maddy. This stuff could just as easily be sprinkled on the open vegetables and fruit at a grocery store. It may not kill as quickly, but you'd sure as heck send the country into panic mode." Justice and the corpses in the room remained quiet for Cade to think. It took the investigative brain a few extra seconds to fully process the information, because he had paused to consider that Dr. Justice had begun calling him by his first name, not title. Once caught up with Justice's offered scenario, he couldn't keep his thoughts inside his head.

"So based on this guy's obvious education, skills, privacy and access to all these ingredients and cooking supplies, he probably ain't living in the projects. But his mixture hasn't left the 'hood. That's probably on purpose I guess." Justice knew Cade was thinking out loud but offered a suggestion to push along the progress.

"If this wackjob killed a soccer mom or straight-A's kid from the suburbs, the media would be even more aggressive, the public would be ticked and they'd all demand immediate answers. But nobody cares about these guys, Maddy." Cade stared through Seis, still in thought.

"Agent Cade?" Cade broke his stare and looked into the serious stare of Dr. Justice. "What if these fools are just being used as a warm up for something much bigger?"

"I care about them," Cade said, ignoring the question and commenting instead on Justice's previous bold statement.

"Do you? Or are you just paid to care about them?"

Cade actually considered the question. He didn't have an immediate answer, and luckily, it was a rhetorical question. Cade left the basement of Cooper Green with his head swirling.

CHAPTER 6

As much as Cade enjoyed Taco Bell, he could not stomach a burrito after his meeting with Justice. He would have to cancel lunch with Esposito. He picked up his cell phone before remembering a personal visit was required for conversation with Esposito.

The phone vibrated in Cade's hand to signal a missed call while he was underground with Justice. The phone's caller ID display showed the number of the dispatch room of the West Precinct. Cade headed toward Uncle Frank's as he placed his return call. Luckily, the familiar voice of Officer Preston answered.

"West Precinct. Officer Preston."

"Hey, Regi, you trying to get me?"

"Is this Special Agent Cade?" Cade did not reply. "Hello?" Cade decided Preston just would not get over the formality.

"Yes, Officer Preston, badge number 1-2-3-4, this is Special Agent Cade. How can I help you?" Preston did not even understand the sarcasm.

"Sir, I was just going to let you know I have been unsuccessful identifying that twenty-eight on your Cadillac." Cade was disappointed, but he knew that showing his frustration would not be accepted well by the officer. After all, Preston's job description did not include helping the feds in the first place.

"Hey, man, thanks for trying. I'll catch you later." He heard the officer saying something other than goodbye as he began to hang up the phone. He returned the phone to his ear.

"Agent Cade?"

"Yeah, go ahead, dude."

"Actually, I may have another lead for you, sir." Cade didn't respond immediately, but chose to quietly soak in the feeling of going from one lead to zero and then back to one in five seconds.

"It may be nothing, but a detective on the early shift reminded me of a late model Cadillac over at a known crack house in Pratt City on Second Avenue. The five hundred block. There's a dead end street running behind the train tracks. I've never seen the thing move, so it's probably not your car, but it would be pretty close to your last scene. I wouldn't try going in there alone. "

Cade wrote the address in the palm of his hand and paid no attention to the warning. He ended the conversation while thinking he'd have to give Officer Preston some cheap federal handout the next time he saw him.

Within minutes of the roller coaster call from Preston,

Cade's phone rang again. He hesitated answering when he saw the zero that came up in the Caller ID when Veida called. It was the same hesitation as a kid pausing before opening that report card.

"Hey," is all Cade offered.

"I guess you're expecting the bad news, or you'd sound a bit more upbeat," Veida said. Cade knew her search was a bust, too, and didn't even ask for more information.

"You're not gonna get that bonus I was gonna put you in for," Cade said, already in the process of ending the disappointing conversation. Only minutes after making a mental note to start saying goodbye, Cade hit the *end* button while hearing some support being offered by his agency liaison and support provider.

Cade had only the newly identified Cadillac to focus on in the case he had decided to officially begin calling the *Doctor LNU* case. That's police speak for "last name unknown." He hoped Justice was right about the suspect having a title of doctor. Not because it would help him solve the case, but because it would be the first and only thing he knew about the murder suspect. Somehow, this made him feel closer to the killer.

Cade drove down Highway 78 toward Pratt City with his stomach growling and mind churning. He was almost certain the new lead was nothing to get excited about, but it would at least give him a way to exert some energy. The shiny black Suburban turned down Second Avenue and its driver instantly knew it was a mistake.

The end of the dead end street was visible, so the target house was within view, but without the aid of binoculars, it wasn't possible to determine which house had the Cadillac parked in front. Most of the homes had cars parked in the front yard. A couple had hoods raised and one was perched on cement blocks. He threw the car in reverse and decided backing up twenty feet would attract less attention than pulling into and out of a driveway.

Officer Preston was certainly right about the inability of putting eyeballs on the house. The closest he could sit was two blocks from the intersection of Second Avenue and the unnamed dead end street. Even seeing a car go in or out wouldn't guarantee it was headed to or from the house with the Cadillac.

Within ten minutes, three young men, two black and one white, made their way out of their respective homes or hangouts in an obvious effort to check out the outsider. The black males were both wearing baseball hats pulled low and slightly twisted to one side. The white male wore the latest in sleeveless shirt fashion. He imagined his daughter calling it a *wife beater*. No surveillance trick was appropriate here. This would not work without some major reinforcements.

It was high noon. The idle of the engine seemed as loud as gunfire in this neighborhood. The engine was shut down, which killed the radio and also stopped the air conditioner. It was a race to see if curious residents or the oncoming warm and uncirculated air would be the first to drive Cade away. Heat lost in the first round.

Cade was a hostage to the surveillance situation. He couldn't get closer to the target in his SUV, and he couldn't leave the SUV to face certain scrutiny and possible vandalism. Twenty minutes of wasted day ended with nothing accomplished. Maybe instead of major reinforcements, he could drum up some minor reinforcement through the help of a man who could maneuver in and around this scene better than a trained agent.

On the short drive to Uncle Frank's, several plans, some more far-fetched than others, crept through Cade's mind. Most of them involved dumping Esposito off near the target location with instructions to get a tag number off the Cadillac. But he knew any plan involving Esposito must include more specific rules and a short leash.

After sitting for fifteen minutes in front of Uncle Frank's, Cade lightly knocked on the door and slowly stepped inside. Uncle Frank was watching another baseball game. The Classic Channel logo in the corner of the screen indicated the game was played some time ago. Still, Uncle Frank sat glued to the screen. The Braves were leading what seemed to be a boring game. Cade found it hard to begin the conversation and just stared at the man until he initiated.

"Hey, Billy. Is Angelo not out there? Maybe he left for school." It hadn't occurred to Cade during the previous meeting that Uncle Frank may be losing his mind. Even if Uncle Frank could carry on a normal conversation, Cade wouldn't be much for talk because he felt like he should be hammering drywall or sweeping the floor for his old friend's uncle.

"Angi!" Mr. Esposito yelled out, nearly causing Cade to jump. After a double play and change of hitters, Uncle Frank shouted again. "I don't know where the little jackass is. Go tell him to come home."

Cade felt obligated to sit for a few minutes, although it wasn't clear if Uncle Frank knew he had company. Cade enjoyed the quiet, but the air from the floor fan was nothing but a gentle warm breeze by the time it reached the agent. Uncle Frank was the first to break the silence again with a surprising comment.

"There's my boy, number ten, here he goes!" Uncle Frank shouted as he scooted forwarded on the edge of his chair. Cade, not a huge baseball follower, realized immediately Frank was referring to Atlanta Braves' superstar third baseman, Chipper Jones, who wore the same number as Frank's nephew.

"I bet you a quarter he hits a homer," Cade put on the table, but Uncle Frank tuned him out. It would have been a risky bet for Uncle Frank, because Cade had already recognized the game as one played nearly ten years prior, which featured Jones leading a Philadelphia Phillies slaughter by hitting two homeruns, one from each side of the plate. He gave time for Chipper to jog around the bases to the cheers of thousands. Cade wondered if Uncle Frank was living some athletic dream of Angelo's that never came to fruition.

Cade returned to his SUV, with nothing more than a wave which was not returned by Uncle Frank. He looked over his SUV and decided it now looked a little like what a pedophile may drive. He waited twenty minutes longer than he would wait at a doctor's office or for a table at any restaurant. He sat in the driveway and watched two drug transactions and one prostitute searching for a quick buck in broad daylight. Cade walked back to the house to leave a message of dissatisfaction with Uncle Frank. He knew he needed to return to his files to catch up from the hour of wasted day.

Before knocking on the door, Cade looked through the cracks in the wall holding the broken windows in place. He could see that Uncle Frank had fallen asleep. He left for civilization without leaving a message. Maybe he'd make it home early two nights in a row, and the family would be surprised.

Leaving the Second Avenue Cadillac untouched for the day would at least give h i m something to think about; even though he knew it was a one-in-a-million possibility.

Cade reached the house and found it empty except for Georgia, who acted like he'd been gone a week. He called Kelly on her cell only to find that she and the kids had made dinner plans. She hadn't considered calling because he was seldom around for dinner.

"That's cool. I'll just take a shower and straighten up a little."

"That'd be great, thanks. We've got some school errands to run too, so we may be a while." Cade and Kelly both knew he wouldn't straighten up the house. The comment was more of a way to let his wife know he acknowledged he participated less and less in domestic chores and needed to do more.

After a quick shower to wash away the visit with the medical examiner, Cade opened the door to his makeshift home office. It was a space in the garage that should be used for family entertaining, but he had needed the room temporarily two years prior for the daily review of a mountain of evidence. It was the same evidence he had used to request the rental of a local storage unit, which for a week, he used as an off-site office. After only four back-to-back dreary days in the drab storage unit, he began relocating furniture and filing cabinets to his unofficial home office. The only thing that remained in the storage unit was a safe, a shredder, a half-empty bottle of Captain Morgan and every government form known to mankind.

He began looking over the photos and reading the autopsy reports of four of the seven victims. He thought about Justice's words and wondered if something big was brewing. Cade *Googled* ricin and pentachlorophenol. What a nasty combination. He thought he should have asked Justice for a percentage of how sure he was on the ingredient list.

"Are you down there, Daddy?" a faint voice asked. Cade looked at his watch and realized the quick visit to his office had somehow lasted nearly two hours. The little man slowly pushed open the office door. Donavan rarely visited his dad's office.

"What's up, Bruce Lee?" Cade asked, recognizing his son's most recent blue belt promotion at the local Tiger Rock Martial Arts Academy. Donavan always returned a look indicating he did not know this "Bruce" fellow.

"Mommy said I could come see you. Is that ok?"

"Sure, buddy. Why wouldn't that be ok? Why don't we hang out a little before bedtime?" Cade asked as he looked around the room to spot items and photos that he should avoid letting his son see. It was too late.

"Who are those men?" Donavan asked, as he climbed up in his father's lap.

"Those are some men who ate something that made them sick. Daddy's trying to find the other man who made the stuff that got them sick."

"Is he a bad man, Dad?"

"Well, he might be, or it could be an accident that I just need to help get straight." Cade never liked to focus on the "bad men." He didn't want Donavan, or even Donavan's older sister, Madelyn, to dwell on these things too long.

"If a man did feed them other men some food that made them sick, that's real bad, right?"

"Yep," Cade said, as he kissed his son's head and thought about what a sensitive kid he was. "You care about all those guys, don't you?"

"Yeah, Daddy, 'cause I'm gonna be a police like you, and we care about people that get hurt."

"Let's go see Mommy. You can sleep in my spot tonight."

Cade helped Donavan climb up on his side of the bed. Kelly barely moved. She grabbed her husband gently and asked if Donavan should sleep in his own bed for the night. Cade loved the insinuation and missed her so much, but he needed just a few more minutes to think things through. He kissed her on the cheek, and she told him goodnight.

Georgia followed Cade back to his office and watched her alpha male settle in his old reclining chair which looked like it should be in a grandmother's living room, not a federal agent's office, official or otherwise. She sat at his feet and whined for attention. He looked at her wrinkled face. She could be the twin sister of Hooch in that old Tom Hanks' movie. Cade stopped rubbing her, and she settled under his feet. He leaned back in the chair and stared at the victim photos with his hands clasped behind his head. She gently licked his toes and he barely noticed.

'Cause I'm gonna be a police like you. Cade heard his son's words again in his mind. He also heard the words of Justice. *Do you? Or are you just paid to care about them?* Cade actually spoke out loud. "Holy crap! This guy isn't screwing with the public, he's screwing with *us!*"

Cade hit Veida on his speed dial before he finished the sentence. "It's Maddy. Here's the favor of the day. It's close to midnight, so I don't know if this counts against yesterday or today's favor count. I need to see if that statewide shared complaint database really works. I need any complaints where the complainant prefix *doctor* box is checked. Also run the name fields in case they listed MD or PhD. If you find one, run all vehicles registered. You're the man! I'll be twiddling my thumbs in the morning waiting for your call."

Cade slipped back to bed about an hour after Kelly's wasted proposition. Georgia settled in on Cade's side of the bed, sighed and closed her eyes. Cade did the same.

Between Justice's words and Donavan's assisted epiphany, Cade stirred most of the next few hours. Esposito was also on his mind, but he couldn't decide if it was because he cared about Esposito or if he was only trying to figure out how to use him to gather information in the places he couldn't visit.

The alarm vibrated the night stand well before six the next morning. He was already awake.

CHAPTER 7

Cade made his better half a pot of coffee. Mainly, it was to kiss up for his actions the night before, but the night wasn't much different from all the others. Cade felt rushed and hurried. Although he had a lot to think about, he really had nowhere to go without a call from Veida.

He logged into his personal e-mail to check his daily incoming solicitations. No mail, of course, just ads. He rarely got a message of value, but he still checked daily. It did manage to kill ten minutes. He also noted he had no Facebook notifications of friend requests. His friend count was hovering around a disappointing fifty.

He also read the news headlines so he wouldn't be totally caught off guard if the sky was falling or the coroner's office was making another statement. After reading nothing of value, he began making his morning pick-me-up. The perfected triple shot, non-fat, no foam latte was a daily must. The hissing sound of the frothing nozzle and smell of over-roasted espresso filled the kitchen. The sound and smell would probably penetrate the bedroom within minutes, waking Kelly, who would then begin her day of super mom duties. He'd be long gone by then.

Cade pulled into Esposito's mom's driveway well before 7 a.m. He knew he'd wasted a good hour of his day. He was looking for a man who wouldn't be up at seven o'clock in the morning unless he hadn't yet gone to bed. Cade started writing a report that was due a week earlier. He thought writing reports in Esposito's driveway was just as good as writing reports anywhere else. He finished his latte and changed the radio station, wasting time until he saw some movement.

Only forty-five minutes passed before he caught a glimpse of activity. It was Mama Esposito in her robe. She had slipped out to feed the dogs. The dogs had been on the porch the entire time without any warning of his encroachment on the property. Esposito's mom waved briefly. Her son must have briefed her on the reunion because she seemed maybe a little embarrassed, but not perturbed at the sight of the big SUV in her driveway. Maybe she just didn't like being spotted in her robe before breakfast.

Cade sat for another thirty minutes wondering if Esposito got the word that he was waiting. Finally, after sitting for a solid hour and fifteen minutes, Esposito emerged. He had orange juice in one hand and a bowl of some breakfast creation in the other. He hopped up on the passenger seat with a "morn," spoken as if the two were back in high school and spending hours upon boring hours with each other in the halls of WBCS.

"Before you say anything, Maddy, I got a great lead on a job yesterday at the parts place. That's where I was. I can ride my bike there, so no more tickets. I feel good, man." Cade paused to be sure Esposito had finished before speaking his calculated words.

"A job would be great, Ang." Cade assumed that Esposito had probably heard enough criticism and coaching. Maybe this situation called for being a listener and even a cheerleader, but he had to vent a bit. "Just don't run off on your new employer like you do Uncle Frank, or it may be the shortest employment that place has ever seen. And really, Taco Bell would be a better job."

"Taco Bell?" Esposito questioned.

"Yeah, I figure you should get a job somewhere that I like to eat. That way you can pay me back in cash or food for the time I'm spending sitting around waiting on you."

Esposito ignored the comment and continued explaining, in too much detail, the opportunity at the parts store located just two blocks from his mother's home. He added that he decided to leave Uncle Frank's house. The less than free roam at his mother's house was a greater distance from the drug addicts and temptation loitering at and around Uncle Frank's.

"I'm feeling great, Mad, and a lot of it is because you took the time to find me. I have my interview this afternoon, so keep your fingers crossed." The tone in

Esposito's voice suggested he wasn't going to be up for lunch later. The lack of a lunch partner meant Cade would have five more dollars to spend on himself, but more importantly, maybe he could focus on the Cadillac which was hopefully still parked and longing for attention.

"Okay, look, I'll keep my fingers crossed for you all day if you'll help me on a lead. It won't take long."

"Do I get a badge," Esposito said, almost before Cade finished the request.

"No, but I'll get you a nice plaque if you don't get me killed." Esposito didn't answer. He seemed to be getting focused for any task that may be assigned.

"I'm looking at a house in Pratt, off Second Avenue. It's a dead end street behind that burned down house."

"That's a war zone back there, man. You'll get your skinny butt stabbed in a minute."

"That's why you're going instead." Esposito stared at Cade. The look on his face was saying *I'll take that challenge*, and not that he was thinking about the danger. "We need new wheels," Cade said, as he motioned toward Esposito's mom's car.

"Let's just do it, man!" Esposito said, nearly shouting. His adrenalin booster had already kicked in with the thought of investigative work. He slammed the door and the sound apparently made him think logically for a moment. "Oh jeez, we can't go in this tank."

Esposito jumped from the Suburban without explanation or mission clarification from Cade. After less than thirty seconds inside his mother's house, Esposito jumped off the porch with car keys in hand. Cade took his gun, baton and two sets of handcuffs as he gave in to the wackiest idea he'd had in months.

After only brief discussion and no real game plan, Cade crawled into the trunk of Mama Esposito's 2002 Chevy Caprice. The missing taillight served as a portal from what would otherwise be total darkness with the trunk closed. Esposito, with a second wave of adrenalin, causing poorly thought out actions, widened the hole in the taillight with the heel of his shoe. Pieces of plastic shattered and spread across the driveway.

Cade's mind was too busy sending signals of *stop* to focus on anything related to an actual investigative plan.

"I need ten bucks in case I get caught up in something?"

"We ain't going shopping."

"What else am I supposed to say I'm doing if I run into somebody? House hunting?" Cade begrudgingly retrieved the ten dollar bill which had been reserved for Taco Bell and gave it to Esposito.

The trunk slammed inches from Cade's head. He tried to get comfortable as he listened to the sounds of Esposito rushing around. He heard the worn out door hinge and then the tired engine turn over. He wanted to yell out for Esposito to slow down and be careful, but fear and isolation just told him to hold on. *Stupid. Stupid. Stupid.* Cade's hope not to get killed was actually not as strong as his hope that nobody found out about this stupid idea.

The car came to a quick stop after only a few minutes and Cade knew they hadn't made it a mile from the Esposito driveway. He rolled onto his side and turned his head for a view of the surroundings. Before he could see out the tiny window, the blue and red reflecting lights made their way inside the darkness. *Oh Jesus, the cops.*

"Mr. Esposito," the unidentified voice said. The tone in the officer's voice, and the fact that he knew Esposito without looking at any identification, were both incredibly bad signs.

"I'm happy for you, man," the officer said in a cool police voice. He was now out of Cade's sight. Cade listened over the pounding of his heart to hear the conversation.

"Why, did I finally win that free lunch drawing at the KFC?"

"No, but you must have gotten your license back, 'cause I know you're not stupid enough to drive on my streets suspended. Get out of the car, jerkwad."

"Officer Shores, I'm finally doing good, man." Cade was following along, but without seeing if Esposito needed the prompting of the officer's name tag, he didn't know if the two had a history.

"You ain't doing good, moron, if you're driving on my road without a license. What's in your pockets?" Cade prayed nothing was in his pockets, or he'd experience the scariest post-arrest car inventory in history when officers back at the impound lot opened the trunk.

"Look, I'm staying out of trouble and I'm clean. I'm going over to clean out a guy's gutters for fifty bucks. Can you give me a break, man? Come on, you know me."

"Yeah, I know you're a doper and a liar. But, I'll give you a break anyway. I'll help you stay clean by taking this ten dollars you had in your pocket that I'll bet you were taking to Pratt City to buy a little rock with, you lying piece of crap."

The three seconds of silence meant Esposito actually knew when to keep his mouth closed. Maybe they'd get out of this one alive. Cade found himself on the other side of the law suddenly, pulling against the *good guys*. He was learning a lesson he never would have admitted before; that maybe the cops aren't always the good guys after all.

The officer, now with lunch money of his own, released Esposito to catch again another day. Cade felt the need for a post-event debriefing or at least a discussion, but maybe it wasn't a big deal to Esposito. Maybe this was the kind of thing people in Esposito's position expected from the police. No wonder it was so hard to drum up witnesses at a crime scene. Cade's frustration was interrupted by another stop. The quick sound of the door opening was a scary thing. If Esposito was jumping out for another police stop, he was certainly about to get shot.

Cade stared into the darkness. He heard birds chirping and felt a strange calmness. The sounds of

Esposito's footsteps through gravel sent Cade to his belly for a better angle and a view through the opening. A piece of red plastic had broken and fallen over the hole, making the already limited view now rose-colored. The sound of a knock immediately followed by the opening of a flimsy metal door sent a wave of nausea through Cade.

"Hello, hello. Anybody here?" Cade heard. He also heard an empty echo in return.

Not only was Esposito in the lion's den, he had left Cade with a rosy but clear view of a beautiful weeping willow tree, and not a thing more. Seconds felt like minutes. Cade remained still and listened to the birds in the distance. The only other sound was that of his heart beating. He was sure someone standing in the driveway would be able to hear it. He was not used to being behind the scenes, and the change in status brought on a touch of anxiety that could only be overcome by fresh air.

Cade maneuvered onto his back and brought his knees to his chest. The tight fit of the trunk wouldn't allow for a kick, but he had plenty of leverage to push against the old trunk with his feet. He felt for the butt of his pistol, and prayed he wouldn't have to draw it after the noise he was about to cause by breaking the old trunk's latch. After twenty agonizing seconds, Cade released his legs and lay still. It might as well be a coffin he thought.

The silent darkness led to panic, which created a dose of extra adrenalin for another escape attempt. He slid around and put his feet against the worn out springs of the back seat. With only half the energy he wasted on the trunk, he broke the plastic connectors holding the seat in place. He rolled across the dirty cushions tearing his shirt in two places. The gun was held at low ready before he even realized he'd pulled it from its holster.

Cade raised his head slightly above the protection of the door frame for a view. The Cadillac was six feet away, but based on its condition, he instantly knew it was not *the* car, and thus, this predicament was top on his list of asinine tricks. He was a sitting duck.

After crawling over the center console, he grabbed the door release and slid out the driver's side in one fluid motion. He sat close to the car, using the wheel as cover, and scanned the area for threats. It was eerily calm. He took a deep breath and said, "Jesus." There was no time for a full-on prayer.

As usual, without careful thought, Cade bolted from the protection of the old Caprice and ran around the useless Cadillac. With nothing else to focus on, he aimed his weapon at the screen door. The darkness behind the screen suggested the front door was open, but he knew the front door wasn't an option.

The side of the old house was cluttered with trash and broken bottles. The backyard was much of the same, but was protected by a thick layer of briars and bushes. He found a safe spot under a window and crouched against the brick home. He hit the magazine release of his weapon for a quick bullet count. He'd been known to be lazy after firearms qualifications and only load a few rounds in an effort to rush range departure for a return to his cases. Today, he may need all thirteen bullets.

Cade tried to control his breathing which had turned into more of a panting. The sound of his breathing was overtaken by a voice, but not Esposito's. He tilted his head toward the sky and saw the open window above him. The open window was a threat, but not as much as the back door, which also stood wide open. The darkness inside the home meant anyone inside could see out, but he couldn't see in from his position.

Cade crawled onto the edge of the nasty back porch, which was covered with glass, needles and the distinct smell of urine. He pointed his gun into the darkness of what appeared to be a kitchen. He crawled across the porch and crouched by the back door.

With the nose of his gun leading the way, he quickly moved his head for a glimpse inside and returned to the protection of the brick. His brain processed what his eyes captured, which was nothing of value. He could still hear the voices, and now identified one as Esposito's. The tone of the conversation sounded friendly. He assumed a drug transaction was taking place in the bedroom down the hall. A new noise was heard - a car - with hip hop blaring through open windows and getting closer. *Oh no! This is not gonna be good,* Cade thought.

The second look inside the home was more controlled, more focused. After determining the only occupants of the small home were Esposito and one other person down the hallway, Cade stepped onto the linoleum-covered floor of the kitchen. The oven door was open and two of the stove's burners were glowing red. He actually considered turning them off.

Through the front door screen, across the open living room of the small home, he saw the quickly-approaching car and had to assume it was headed his way. The ramifications would not form in his head. He moved quickly but quietly down the hall. He pulled his gun close to his chest as trained, so as not to announce his presence too soon. Shooting one man and running through the woods would be easier than a four on one gunfight in the front yard.

Three doors led from the hall; one bathroom and two bedrooms. He approached the end of the hallway without the slightest noise. The conversation was becoming clear now, and it was not a drug transaction.

Cade saw his target through the small gap between door and door frame. He stretched out the pistol and brought it on target. He nudged the door further open with the end of the gun and stepped dangerously close to the target.

When Esposito opened his eyes, the weapon was aimed inches from his head. He didn't move. He sensed no danger from Cade, but he was unaware of the threat that was certainly seconds away. Car doors slammed in the distance. *One, two, three, four* subjects at least, Cade counted in his head. Esposito, focused only on the present, smiled.

The gun stayed on target, aimed directly at the back of her head. She was wearing next to nothing and appeared to be just leaning against Esposito. Maybe it started as a hug, or kiss even, but she just stood now, her head against Esposito's bare chest. Cade did not even take the time to wonder how Esposito became shirtless in less than five minutes.

He moved close enough to the woman to touch the back of her greasy blonde hair with the blue steel barrel of the gun. She blinked her eyes a few times, as if she had been sleeping in Esposito's embrace, and slowly turned to face the barrel of Cade's weapon. Her eyes fought to stay open and her head bobbled like a McDonald's Happy Meal toy.

"Hey baby," she said, as she reached out toward Cade. The gun pressed against her nose. She was high as a kite. Cade looked into the eyes of the woman who he immediately felt was void of emotion or feeling, like she was hollow and soulless. Esposito stood, his lean and tanned upper torso exposed.

"Hey baby," she said again, louder and more slurred than the first time. Cade holstered his weapon and put his hand forcefully over her mouth. She was a walking zombie and had no energy to put up a fight. He pushed her into the closet. The floor was covered with pieces of mail, certainly stolen from nearby mailboxes, and garbage bags full of clothes. The latter of which broke her fall.

"They're coming!" Cade shouted.

"Who's coming?"

"The Prize Patrol, genius, who do you think? Get your scrawny butt out that window."

The front door flew open and what sounded like an entire football team filled the tiny living area. Esposito was struggling with the approximate five foot jump. Cade put his hand on Esposito's backside and pushed him out the window to the dry mud below. With another look to the closet, and the sleeping crack princess inside, Cade followed.

The escapees made it to the cover of the Cadillac. The car-full of men were now inside and most likely demanding answers about the strange car in the front yard. The Caprice was only feet away.

"If they took the keys, I'm running for it and you can buy your mama another car. On three."

Esposito didn't seem to notice he was topless until he made it to the car. Cade fumbled with the keys as two of the men barreled back out of the target house with guns raised.

"Get down!" Cade yelled, but Esposito needed no warning. He was nearly on the floorboard already.

The Caprice started like a champ and threw rocks from the rear tires as it fishtailed back onto the paved road. The two men returned to the interior of the home in an apparent attempt to retrieve keys. Cade didn't look back.

"I left my shirt, man."

"I'll buy you a new one or you can go back

tomorrow."

"No, it had my name in it" Esposito said with a laugh as if he didn't just nearly get killed. "Seriously man, were you watching? I was about to make my move."

Cade rushed to get Esposito back home in time to make it to his interview, hoping all the time it was an actual interview, not something created for conversation.

CHAPTER 8

A new parking spot was created for the Caprice behind the Esposito home in case the Second Avenue boys somehow recognized Esposito or did a drive by.

"Keep your head down for a few days. If you ever tell anybody what just happened, I'll kill you myself." Esposito returned to the safety of his home as if this sort of thing happened every day. Cade's heart didn't slow to normal speed until he was nearly home. He was officially off early. Although it seemed like he'd just spent hours in a gun battle, it wasn't even noon. The house was quiet.

After a shower and a thirty minute power nap, Cade's thoughts were clear enough to realize how lucky he was to have escaped Pratt City. The experience actually motivated him to put Dr. LNU on hold for the rest of the day to clean up other matters that could get him in administrative hot water.

Cade visited the warehouse and spent an hour shredding old intelligence reports that should have been shredded months prior. He accounted for evidence in three of his cases that he thought might have been lost. Finally, he decided to spend the afternoon focusing on a case that had been lingering and would certainly raise questions should his boss conduct a review and find that nothing had happened on the case in over a month.

After clearing a few cobwebs, he returned to his mobile office and headed downtown to advance, or possibly close, a less-volatile drug cases. The case involved the worst kind of drug dealer, one wearing a coat and tie. It was a move of strategy and not retreat, Cade told himself. He would get rid of this case in the event of another clue or dead body showing up and requiring his full attention.

The white collar case, which had taken a backseat to Doctor LNU, involved an executive at a large downtown bank. The suspect was allegedly selling drugs which were smuggled home by his wife. The co-suspect was a nurse at the University Hospital. The case got labeled as a possible terrorism matter after a pill bottle ended up in the inventory of an arrestee charged in a domestic terrorism bomb plot. Cade hadn't wasted energy fighting what everyone knew was a bad case labeling.

There was no evidence and no credible witnesses. There had been one statement from a high school senior. The kid wanted to clear his conscience by confessing his appetite for steroids to impress college scouts. Steroids led to his consumption of morphine to deaden the pain resulting from over-zealous workouts. The morphine led to his pain medication addiction which led to his purchase of a quantity of drugs from the youngest senior VP the bank ever had on payroll.

The kid was a good witness. At least he *was* a witness right up until the time of his overdose and death. For the sake of the kid, Cade had kept the case open with no leads, but he would close it today, one way or another.

Cade glided past security in the lobby with a quick flash of his badge. He made it past the secretary guarding the main lobby of the Investments Bureau on the twenty-sixth floor of the Vulcan National Building.

He used the tried and true method of building entry taught by his late grandmother. He visualized walking down the corridors of the Graysville, Alabama Long Branch Hospital with her when he was eleven and too young to visit his great-grandmother in intensive care. *Just act like you own the place, Mad-Mad,* Mit had whispered to him.

A voice brought Cade back from the sterile tile floor of the Long Branch Hospital to the plush carpeted hallway of the bank building.

"Hello, may I help you?" asked the young, attractive woman on guard. Cade never broke stride. He smiled at the young beauty who stood a good inch taller than him.

"No thanks. Bob just called for me." He was betting there was some Bob working somewhere on the floor, or at least the young lady would think about it long enough to allow him to slip into the fabric of the office.

The ingrained Southern hospitality possessed by the hall monitor would prevent her from confronting such a friendly intruder. He snatched two blank notebooks from the top of a vacant cubicle and hastened his pace as if rushing to a meeting. No one interrupted what appeared to be a motivated and busy bank employee.

It took Cade less than five minutes to find the corner office of Mr. Dunstan Lawson. He swooped right in as if Lawson had called him for a meeting.

"Hey, Dunstan, I've been meaning to ask if you're related to Garrett Lawson." Lawson looked puzzled but would use the question as a stall tactic in effort to recall just who the intrusive man was.

"No, I don't think so," Lawson said. Then after a lengthy, uncomfortable pause, Lawson added, "I'm sorry. Have we met?"

Cade gave him a look as if he should be embarrassed, but then let him off the hook after only a few moments of uncomfortable tension. He often wondered if he had become a law enforcement agent just so he could unleash his sarcasm on unsuspecting sleazy interviewees.

"I like the way you put that, Dunstan. I thought you'd give me the more disrespectful response of *who are you*, which, psychologically, is more harsh because you're striking the key question of life. You know, *who are you* means more like you must have little value because I don't even know who you are. You could have also gone with something like *I don't know you*, which would make me inferior to you. You'd be saying you are more powerful and don't need me, but here I am kissing up to you for something."

Lawson looked as if he expected Cade to laugh and explain the real purpose of barging into the office. Cade sat down in one of the two chairs that faced Lawson, and propped up his feet, putting his new Puma sneakers on top of Lawson's shiny desk.

He grabbed a little tray of tiny magnetic men, wondering if it was a gift or handout at the last company conference. He began speaking while he stacked the little men. His confrontation method was a favorite in his repertoire of suspect interview tactics.

"Look, Dunstan, I'm sure you saw the bulge here. Unfortunately, it's a badge. I bet you were thinking I was just real excited to meet you. Now, I'm not the typical badge wearing kind of guy, all sneaky and stuff. I like to lay it all out there, so here it is. I have three calls from individuals claiming you are selling them drugs. They all say you got the dope from your wife who got it from the hospital. Obviously, I need to confront her, but I thought it'd be easier to see you first. Speaking in your office is a lot more private than leaning over that nurses' station on the second floor of the hospital. And while I do enjoy following people around, digging through their trash, and interviewing their neighbors, something tells me a guy named Dunstan is just the kind of guy you confront man to man. Plus, I heard you had these little guys."

Cade only then looked away from his magnetic

creation to stare at Dunstan. His look said, *go ahead and call somebody*. As if he had received the telepathic message, Dunstan picked up his phone and dialed a number from a card he found in his top desk drawer.

"Rick Jaffe, please," Dunstan said while looking directly at Cade. Cade knew Jaffe as a great defense attorney and great adversary. The two had battled over several high profile cases in the past. Jaffe was a published author and had encouraged Cade to pursue his own book. He had actually included Cade in his first book about the trials and tribulations of a high-paid defense attorney. Jaffe had spent two full pages depicting the antics of an "unorthodox" and "out-of-the-box investigator" on a witch hunt for one of his clients. It was all crap, of course, but a good read none the less.

"Tell Rick it's the guy from Chapter 12, and I want top billing in his next book." Lawson stood as if willing to stand toe to toe with Cade now that he had backup via telephone.

"I want your card," Dunston said with new attitude.

"Get it from your attorney," Cade said over his shoulder as he left Dunstan's office. He was happy to see the front desk attendant back at her post and obviously not on the hunt for him.

"Did you find Bob?" she asked with the most sincere voice.

With a hand on his hip and a slight lisp, he responded, "No, I never made it past Dunstan's office. I was playing with his, um, little men." He knew this would have gotten him in trouble with any other harassee, but Jaffe would find it amusing.

As the elevator doors closed, Cade grabbed the cell phone from his back pocket, the place his daughter, the fashion coordinator, instructed him to carry it. He had felt the vibration of an incoming call while sparring with Dunston but couldn't take the call in the middle of battle. The red light on the cell phone indicated no service in the elevator. He hoped for a lucky find by Veida but feared she'd have nothing.

He occupied his mind by adjusting both framed message boards and the mirror in the elevator on the painfully slow ride down to the lobby. He looked at his reflection in the perfectly leveled mirror and wondered if he looked like a cop, or maybe even an actor after that performance. He wondered how long it would take Jaffee to call and how much he would charge Dunstan to work out a plea to some insignificant charge.

Cade thought about Jaffe's book and the pending work of his newest drug recovering friend and quasi informant. He wondered if anyone else he knew had published a book. The doors opened to the sound of a ding and the sight of two security guards who looked at him as though he was their target.

"What's up fellows? You guys gotta loose cannon on twenty-six," Cade said as he looked at his phone and waited for the light to turn green so he could check for a positive message. Before hitting the call button, he checked the missed call log. It had, in fact, been an attempted call from Veida. The phone vibrated in his hand, signaling a message. He felt apprehensive.

"Hey, it's your number one fan. I just wanted to call before the end of the day 'cause that search is going to take some time. Apparently, you can only do a database search of key words in the comment and name boxes. I checked for titles in the name boxes and found nothing. I'm having to manually scroll through the individual complaints, and only got two days' worth done. I'll see how far I can get tomorrow."

Cade called it quits for the second time in one day. He only had the slightest feeling of success because he hadn't been fired or sued - yet. At least he would be home by dinnertime, which was an unusual treat, and it made for a positive day after all.

Georgia was alone and waiting by the door for her master. Cade remembered it was TaeKwonDo night and he'd missed another class. He called out twice for his daughter, expecting her to be tucked away in her bedroom with the iPod blaring through her ear buds and Facebook chats scrolling across her computer screen. He climbed the stairs, leaving Georgia behind whining. Her hips were growing too old to climb the steep stairs. He knocked twice on her door before opening it slowly to an empty room. She must have gone along to Donavan's class, hoping to cause a stir within the teenage ranks of the martial arts class.

The investigator slipped into investigator mode and

opened the small pink laptop resting on Madelyn's bed. The desktop instantly came to life, indicating it hadn't been shut down too long. After pulling up the hidden files and typing in the password, 1*sentry*, he began scrolling through pages of secretly copied Facebook chats, Internet browsing and Skype history. Nothing of concern. She was a great kid, despite the limited interaction with a watchful and protective father. Georgia announced the arrival of his family, and he sprang from the bed, closing all files and replacing the computer to its exact previous position.

The successful spy mission reminded him how lucky he was, and the positive feelings helped him block out the inner-city for a nice family dinner of Zaxby's, brought home by his thoughtful wife. The kids argued over the extra sauce, Georgia got too many leftovers, and only one drink was spilled. It was great family time.

CHAPTER 9

Cade woke well rested, but as he came around, his brain began to reload all the stress and questions left over from the night before. He did seem to have some needed energy for a day of organizing files and catching up on dreaded paperwork. For nearly six straight hours, Cade waded through the required forms and checklists of case after case. He managed to transfer three cases to other agents in other cities, and to close three headache cases outright. He checked his watch no less than forty times wondering when Veida may call.

He returned the cases he couldn't get rid of back into two metal filing cabinets. The cabinets held all the work justifying his career. All the work that is, except for the Doctor LNU case. It was kept in its very own banker's box. Cade had put the entire contents of the case in the box nearly twenty-four hours earlier. It was an exercise meant to bring about a new view or new ideas when he unpacked the contents.

He removed victim photos first and refashioned his

corkboard with the photos of the six victims prior to Pooky. All were labeled with their gang or *street* names, not their birth names. For the first time, Cade wondered how the parents of the deceased would feel about that, especially the mother of *Big Nasty*.

Solving a case like this required mostly talking. In the past month, Cade had spoken with homeless men who slept in doorways and prostitutes who were always looking up and down streets and alleys. These potential witnesses, often ignored by *regular* people, were hunted by Cade because he recognized their potential. It took constant effort to get these people to talk, but Cade thought maybe giving them some space for a bit would pay off in the long run.

Esposito kept popping into Cade's thoughts. He stopped periodically to call Mrs. Esposito for an update on any Angelo sightings or job announcements. She offered no ideas as to his whereabouts or the outcome of the alleged job interview. He briefly considered calling the Auto Zone but feared he may find that Esposito had exaggerated his odds of landing the auto store job. He dismissed the need to catch up with Esposito right away. He returned to the typing of a reply e-mail related to management's dissatisfaction about one of the previous day's case closings.

Deep in thought, the phone didn't register with Cade until the second ring. He glanced at the Caller ID which signaled another call from a pay phone. Fourth ring. He stopped typing and reached for the phone knowing only one person in his life that made calls from pay phones. Even though Cade had truly been worried about Esposito's whereabouts since the Second Avenue fiasco the day before, he was now agitated and answered in a tone to demonstrate it.

"Are you in a ditch?"

"Hey, Maddy." Cade could detect a lot from just Esposito's two words and tone which said, *I'm in trouble* and *can you help me*? He didn't respond, and the phone was silent. Cade would not speak first, and the silence was uncomfortable. After hearing a yell echoing in the background, he instantly knew Esposito was in a holding cell.

"What precinct?"

"I didn't do it this time, Maddy."

Another probation violation, another probation officer, another amount owed to a court that may never be paid in full. Cade reluctantly climbed into his SUV and drove across town to give a hard-earned two hundred dollars to Mrs. Esposito. Surely, she was more tired than anyone of bailing her son out of jail.

Two hundred dollars was a big deal for Cade. He earned more money in a month than Esposito would see in a year, but because his wife handled the household finances, Cade rarely saw cash. Over the past few years, he had attempted to save a little here and there through travel vouchers. He even took the occasional grocery store *cash back* option which he embezzled from the wife. His modest stash of cash was for the surprise gifts and purchases for his wife that he knew came much too infrequently.

Mrs. Esposito was almost in tears as she thanked Cade. He lied and said it was government money, paid for information provided by her son. He knew the delinquent jail bird would never pay it back anyway, and the story would at least console Mrs. Esposito.

He began to back out of the gravel driveway, but stopped to allow a slowly moving Mustang to pass. The car was mostly blue but it had a red door and was partially covered in rust and bondo. He sized up the driver and two passengers as trouble. He was surprised and maybe a bit frustrated when he saw the car slow in front of the Esposito house. The driver and both passengers studied the house as if they were looking for someone they knew.

Cade decided not to spend too much time deciphering their actions. It didn't take a well-trained investigator to realize Esposito was not out of the pit and these other pit-dwellers were looking for their friend.

Less than an hour passed after Cade returned to his home office before he received the second pay phone call of the day. He tried to remember the last time he used a pay phone. He wondered if he was now suddenly responsible for pay phone income all over the city. The number listed on the phone's mini screen meant it was a call from downtown. He was impressed by the speed of the Jefferson County Jail's outbound processing.

"You out?" Cade said after a pause. Esposito sounded embarrassed and kept his explanations to a minimum. Cade arrived at the jail within the hour. He parked in the back alley, in a space reserved for law enforcement vehicles. He flipped down his visor light and slipped around the building to the busy 20th street. He spotted Esposito across the street by Maria's Deli and figured he was already panhandling or trying to bum a cigarette.

Cade badged his way through lobby security and walked through the beeping metal detector. The Sheriff's Deputy only looked at his watch, and Cade took it as a signal that the officer was more concerned about the quickly approaching five o'clock shift change than he was about a Division Agent.

He proceeded to *Processing* to hear Esposito's arrest details and possible fate. He knew he'd be hearing a much more colorful story from the culprit.

Cade stood in line and listened to the woman in front of him relaying the details of a Failure to Appear charge that shouldn't be held against her son because he was in jail in another city for theft. He briefly considered going back outside to make sure the recently freed man didn't get in more trouble if some cop spotted the city violation of panhandling that Esposito was so good at breaking.

Cade made it to the front of the line. The clerk looked down at the computer screen like Ms. Crabtree in the tenth grade reading how poorly Cade did on the History test but not saying anything.

"Um hm, yep, yep."

"Come on, what's the damage?" Cade pressed but remained as friendly as possible.

"Are you the federal agent?" Cade knew this was trouble.

"I am *a* federal agent. Is it that obvious?" The lady gave him a look that suggested she didn't really care and was just reading the screen until time to go home.

"Says here Mr. Esposito told the arresting officer he was not loitering to buy drugs but was working with a federal agent, trying to get names of drug traffickers. I'm not sure if the low bond was because he was clean, or if it was because of his association to a fed." Cade wondered if that was a question or a comment, so he remained silent and as humble looking as possible. "You can go back to Intake to see the full report. They probably closed at five, but you can show them your badge, and they'll let you back."

"Thanks," Cade said, as he smiled and turned in the direction opposite of Intake and walked back through security to 20th Street.

The drive home was a quiet one. When they arrived at the house, Esposito's mom was sitting on the front porch in the shade. It was an overcast day and the temperature outside was tolerable.

"I'm not mad about the drugs, and I'm not gonna preach to you. I can't understand the hold that drugs have on you because I've never been hooked. To tell you to stop would be a waste of breath. But if you ever use my name again..." Esposito interrupted without turning in his seat to face Cade.

"I never used your name. I said I was gettin' drug information to pass on to a federal agent I met with last week. That ain't a lie, and I didn't use your name."

"Go make up some crap about why they grabbed you this time before your mom walks over here."

Esposito got out without another word, and Cade left for the real world. He drove past the Forestdale Square where vivid memories of Pooky had already started to fade. Cade wondered if Dr. Justice had released the body for burial. He wondered if anybody showed up at the funeral.

Another missed dinner and another sleepless night. Cade turned off his alarm before 5 a.m. the next morning, and left before his family had a chance to complain about the evening before. It was time for another burst of effort toward finding the killer or killers of Pooky and his pals. He was eager to hear from Veida or Lester about any computer searches or any new word on the street.

Cade took less than an hour to sign the last closing document on another less interesting and less significant case. He happily sent it off to the closed file room at his agency headquarters. He looked over his case list which was down to six now. It was a modest number of cases for a fed. It was a case load that would be laughed at by any local or state detective working the streets. Federal cases were much more complex Cade told himself, as if justifying his salary.

The thought of *real* cops made him think of the cops at Pooky's death scene. He grabbed the case file and opened it to see his last entry. It contained scene notes and other information provided by the local detectives. Cade's mind was slowly getting back to full speed. Maybe the short break from the case would be a benefit.

He had become pretty good at turning on and off the sections of his mind used for work. The section storing the Dr. LNU facts was also filled with images of bodies, kids selling drugs, the smell of urine in alleys being searched for clues and witnesses, and death. Another section was for birthday parties, family trips and dreaded visits to Chuck E. Cheese. Maybe that was one reason Esposito kept surfacing in the mental images in Cade's mind. Maybe the memory storing mechanism was struggling with where to put images of Esposito because he had connections to both sides.

He visualized two photos like a police photo spread. The one on the left was Esposito's yearbook photo. The other side stored the mug shot from his first arrest about ten years later. Without close inspection, you'd swear these were photos of two different individuals.

The phone on Cade's desk that used to ring so infrequently brought him back. He checked first for the feared notice of *pay phone* on the caller ID display. Instead, he got a number with a series of zeros, indicating to Cade a government agency's blocked number.

The call was from a dispatcher at the Bessemer Police Department. He instantly pictured Esposito in the back of a Bessemer marked unit.

"Is this Special Agent Cade?"

"No, it's Maddy Cade, what can I do for you?"

"Is this the agent who's working on the doctored drugs?" the caller pressed on quickly.

"Yes, what can I do for you?" Cade responded, sounding a bit more direct and trying to rush the mysterious caller.

"I got a call a while ago from a man who refused to identify himself, saying he took some video surveillance at his house that we may want. He says the video shows the car that ran over that kid. The caller wants to sell the video, I think. He was talking about his street lights or something. He was hard to follow. He wouldn't give too much specific information, so I told him an officer would call him back. My sergeant suggested I call you since the dead guy he's referring to is probably your last victim." Cade let the less than useful information digest a moment.

"Well, I appreciate your sergeant thinking of me, but is there any other information that might help me find this anonymous caller?" he asked without sounding too demanding or sarcastic.

"Oh, yes sir, I have his telephone number, and I pulled a name from the Water Department." Cade pictured Radar from the M*A*S*H television show. Like the officer, Radar would always hold back a piece of information until it was requested, then, in a very naïve manner, would deliver the home run.

CHAPTER 10

Within fifteen minutes, Veida had cross-referenced the name and number, and had confirmed the address and utility records for the only possible Dr. LNU witness, Lawrence Snow. It was a record trip across town. In less than forty minutes, Cade was maneuvering through the trashy street in front of the Snow's residence.

He pulled in front of the small house and noted what appeared to be a late model Nissan Altima. It wasn't a bank-breaking automobile, but certainly not the norm for the neighborhood. The car had a Georgia license plate which Cade discretely copied to the palm of his hand before getting out to face the muggy air.

Before knocking on the door, Cade walked the long way around the front porch, as he was trained to do. He looked through as many cracks and window openings as possible. He felt no threat, but kept a safe distance from the front door. The door opened so fast it sent Cade's thumb to the safety lock on his weapon. His experience and instinct gave him the reserve to leave it holstered.

The occupant, presumed to be Lawrence Snow, was holding a piece of carpet folded into a makeshift dustpan. The rushed motion of the man was an effort to clean what Cade could immediately see was an empty house. The man was startled by Cade and seemed to be a bit paranoid. Cade presented his badge to the man and said in his most calming voice, "Mr. Snow?"

"Who are you?" the man asked, which struck Cade as a peculiar greeting.

"I'm Maddy Cade. I'm following up on your call to the Bessemer Police Department." Cade was interrupted by the man who now seemed more of a suspect than a witness.

"I didn't call the police, but I'm calling them now. I don't know who you are. I could get a badge like that anywhere." Cade realized that his street attire looked anything but *police.* But what the man had in the area of fashion sense, he obviously lacked in everyday walking around brains. The man reentered the old house and slammed the door behind him.

Cade prided himself on his communication abilities and rational thinking. He knocked on the window nearest the door. The man, now agitated, pulled back the bent and stained blinds.

"Can you just raise the window a bit and let me talk with you?" The man could hear Cade very well through the cheap, single pane window. Cade could see a telephone in the man's hand as he firmly pressed the blinds back against the window.

"Not without a warrant, I won't!" Cade took a moment to enjoy the man's words and the unusual attempt at a conversation. Cade often interacted with people whose late-night police show viewing taught them just enough police lingo and procedure to make bold and humorous proclamations, like, "I want my phone call now" or, "Not without a warrant, I won't." Cade's instincts did not shout *danger* but *get your own cops here!*

Cade flipped open his cell phone and hit the number two button of his speed dial. Luckily, Lester was on duty and was "on standby" nearby. Cade knew that meant he was taking a nap somewhere shady.

Lester arrived just seconds before the unit that was dispatched as the result of Mr. Snow's call. Although Lester was outside his assigned territory, he easily flagged off the arriving officer who considered it a lucky break and didn't even ask why Lester responded.

Mr. Snow, seeing the marked unit in his driveway, re-emerged to begin his opening argument. Lester looked away twice to avoid laughing directly at Mr. Snow. After a few minutes of patiently hearing Mr. Snow talk about crime, inoperable street lights, low police presence and barking dogs, Lester convinced Mr. Snow that Cade was on the up and up. It took another thirty minutes of well-played dialog and two against one conversation before Mr. Snow admitted to his initial call regarding still photos, not video, as had been reported by the police department. Lester did the best he could to follow along in the conversation and did a fine job acting as if he had an interest in the matter.

Once Mr. Snow was in a semi-participating mode, Lester motioned to Cade that he needed to return to the streets. Cade knew Lester couldn't stay out of service too long without explanation to the dispatcher. As Lester turned to his marked unit, Cade realized how much he missed spending time with one of his few friends. Looking over Mr. Snow's shoulder, Cade could see Lester holding his outstretched little finger and thumb by his ear, making the universal hand gesture for *call me*. Mr. Snow kept on rambling and didn't seem to notice that it was now just the two men talking.

Cade used all his energy to bring the man to a spot in conversation useful to the case. The man, who Cade now called Larry, had no knowledge of the Dr. LNU investigation. His call was merely an effort to increase police visibility around his newly inherited house. He was desperate to keep drug pushers and prostitutes away long enough to dump his father's real estate.

Larry stumbled and sputtered so much that Cade wondered at first if he had some sort of speech impediment. The typical investigator would have interrupted the man by asking follow-up questions, but Cade knew better. He let the man ramble on until he had complained about a laundry list of items in need of repair and attention. Cade agreed, sympathized and even joined with Mr. Snow in protest, until he could zoom in on information related to the photos of the mysterious Cadillac.

The camera was an outdoor, black-and-white version used mostly by hunters trying to track the route of trophy bucks. Larry had duct-taped the camera to the railing on his front porch in an effort to capture "undesirables" using his father's abandoned home for immoral purposes.

Larry explained that, within two weeks of his father's death, vandals had broken the windows and stolen most of the furniture and anything of value. He described the scene when he entered the house nearly a month prior to see five or six "dopers" on the couch and in the floor. Larry proudly described his actions in "kicking their lazy, good-for-nothing butts out the door."

Snow went off on several tangents related to crime and law enforcement in general. Cade fought the urge to speed the story. The man, speaking now with more ease and comfort, explained the photos he captured of the Cadillac parking in his driveway. After forty-five minutes with Snow, Cade finally made the connection between Snow and the Bessemer PD tipoff. It was reassuring to Cade that police departments around the city had their eyes open for complaints related to the Cadillac. Cade finally asked the question he'd been struggling to hold back for nearly an hour.

"So, can we take a look at the photos?"

"Not without protection for my house," Snow said in a demanding voice. Cade sat in disbelief.

"I'll see what I can do."

Cade left within seconds, realizing staying moments too long in Snow's yard would cause him to lose his control with the disturbed man. It caused him great pain to leave without the treasure, and still photos would be just as much treasure as video. But his experience told him that pushing one moment longer could have resulted in losing the possibility of ever recovering the evidence.

He turned the ignition key with his right hand while pressing the keys of his cell phone with his left. He located and redialed the number to the Bessemer Police Department to discuss the finer points of message taking. After being transferred twice and placed on hold for no more than fifteen seconds, Cade closed his phone and threw it in his center console. He left the Snow property no closer to catching a killer than when he'd arrived.

He drove toward home on autopilot. His mind churned through several threats, tricks and bluffs he could have unleashed on Snow. He thought his quick decision to be Mr. Friendly may have been the wrong approach. He hoped for a second chance.

The muffled sound of the cell phone vibration brought Cade out of his trance. After seeing the 615 area code on the face of his phone, he turned his wrist to check the date on the face of his watch. It was time again for a visit from Agent Rich Hartline.

Hartline was an agent from Nashville, Tennessee who served as Cade's firearms instructor. It was not a duty Hartline requested, and he resented the quarterly intrusion to his schedule. The mandatory qualifications were anything but pleasant, but did give Cade four days a year of interaction with another agency employee. Even a frustrated, grumpy agent was a nice change of pace sometimes.

"What's up, man," Cade said, as a greeting and rush of the conversation. He knew the call was only to make sure he would be at the range on time. Hartline wasn't much for conversation. Cade tried to send a tone conveying he was happy about their scheduled day of pistol firing.

"Eight at the county on Wednesday, right." Hartline said, skipping a greeting altogether. It was clearly a statement, not a question.

"Can't wait," Cade said, as his mind shifted back to Snow. The less than personable Hartline just might be his solution. If he failed to manipulate Snow in the morning, he'd use Hartline as Plan B. Cade knew Hartline wouldn't pass on an opportunity to break early from shooting to conduct a confrontational interview with a man as difficult as Snow. He figured he'd just relay to Hartline that Snow said he'd "kick anybody's tail who steps foot on my property without notice." Hartline was always up for a good face off.

The night was another typical one for Cade. Dinner was in the oven, covered with foil, and he made it home just in time to tell the kids goodnight. Sleep was a necessity, but didn't fit into the investigator's schedule.

Cade was up before Georgia who awoke only long enough to look out the window into the darkness. She looked back at Cade as if to tell him his alarm wasn't working properly. The tired agent threw on yesterday's jeans and a hat to speed his departure, but couldn't skip making his caffeine-loaded latte. He crept out of his sleepy neighborhood before increasing to breakneck speed.

During the drive, he thought through a dozen or so scenarios of how to handle Snow. He hoped to find some resolution without having to use another agent. Then again, he did think it would be amusing, in some strange double agent kind of way, to cast Hartline in the role of *bad cop*. He figured Hartline would last about ten seconds before threatening to stomp Snow. He could then swoop in and save Snow from certain pain and win his trust.

Adrenaline and anticipation pumped the caffeine to Cade's heart and brain. He arrived at Snow's and slowly pulled into the gravel drive of what now looked like a vacant house. He was relieved when he spotted the bumper of Snow's Nissan parked beside the dilapidated home. Snow would surely be agitated today if he slept on the bare floor. He waited for nearly twenty minutes, seeing no movement from inside. As was typical for Cade, his impatience caused his mind to begin forming wacky solutions to push things along. He grabbed the first thought that popped into his head.

He slid from the driver's seat, switching the cup

containing the last of his morning homemade latte from his right to left hand. He picked up a golf ball-sized piece of gravel from the driveway. With a brief flashback to his second baseman days at West Birmingham, he flung the rock into the overflowing metal garbage can as if he was turning two in the bottom of the ninth.

A direct hit made a bang that echoed off the old house. He maneuvered the coffee again and jumped back behind the wheel. He rolled his car forward just as Mr. Snow rushed out of the house in search of a drug dealer or prostitute.

"Hey, buddy! Was that you?" Snow yelled, using the term "buddy" as anything but buddy-like. It wasn't clear if Snow remembered Cade.

"Was what me?" Cade answered, doing his best impression of his son when challenged about something.

"You ain't helping me patrolling through here. I need marked units," Snow said in an agitated voice. His memory had finally caught up.

"I'm not driving by for you. I'm actually here to meet with another neighbor. Turns out everybody has cameras rolling these days. One of your neighbors has video. I'm going to review his footage." Snow seemed to accept the concocted story.

"Good, I'm having an investor come by today. If I get a solid offer, I'm going to take it and get out of this place in one piece."

"So, if you don't need protection any more, you

want me to stop all the calling I've been doing?" He figured if Snow believed the last crazy statement, maybe he'd believe two.

"No! Never know about people, they're strange, say one thing and do another. Sometimes people even make up stories for no good reason."

Cade didn't believe Mr. Snow was smart enough to catch his lying, and he was certainly not witty enough to call him out in such repartee. Cade also knew he shouldn't act overanxious about the evidence he so desperately wanted. His mouth opened before knowing what he was going to say.

"Mr. Snow, the other neighbor says the car had an out-of-state license plate. That's the same as yours, right?"

"I don't know" is all Snow would give. "Officer, uh, what was your name again?" Snow asked, as if he'd just remembered the time the two spent chatting just the evening before.

"It's Maddy Cade." Ignoring the suggestion that Cade didn't use titles, Mr. Snow inserted his own. "Well, Officer Cade. I'm thinking you haven't seen this video, and you're here to get my photos." Cade's mind raced for just the right answer. The tables were turned now, and he was the one being asked tough questions and trying not to get caught in a lie.

"No, I'm a little early for our appointment. I told you I'd keep an eye on the house for you, and here I am, eyes and all." Snow seemed to buy it again.

"Well, since you don't need it, I'll tell you I didn't have the whole tag anyway. I just have the first two letters and numbers." Cade was grasping now for anything.

"Yeah, A-G or A-B, something like that. The other neighbor said he has a good picture, but I couldn't make out what he was saying on my cheap government cell phone." Cade looked away from Snow and took an imaginary sip of coffee from his now empty coffee mug.

He looked back at Snow who was looking right into his eyes. He tried to look as unconcerned as possible. Mr. Snow smirked in a way that reminded Cade of the way Hannibal Lector talked to Agent Clarece Starling in *Silence of the Lambs*.

"You're not as good of a liar as you think, Officer Cade." Cade knew he was busted. "If the offer doesn't come through, I'll only be here a few more days." Cade knew he'd lost that exchange, and he left trying not to show rejection. He calmly wished Mr. Snow good luck with the showing.

Cade's knee-jerk reaction was to go get a search warrant for Snow's house, but even he had a hard time with a bold lie in a sworn affidavit for a search warrant. He was creative and pushed every envelope known to man, but to say it was probable that anything was in that house would be a lie. He had just seen the entire thing as bare as could be.

Plan B couldn't fail now. It would be great either way, Cade thought, because either the event would lead

Snow to release information, or the meeting between Hartline and the uncooperative man would be great to watch.

CHAPTER 11

Cade's decision to retreat meant he was out of ideas and energy for the day, and it was barely 8 a.m. Figuring he wouldn't get any more work accomplished, he drove a few miles to Uncle Frank's. Before making it to the dead end street where the sad home stood, Cade spotted Esposito and Skip walking with a young woman.

Esposito saw Cade's large out-of-place vehicle and parted ways with his female friend. Cade pulled alongside Esposito while wondering if he and the young lady were leaving Uncle Frank's after an all-nighter. Skip stood on his rear legs to look in the SUV as the window lowered. Cade, a true dog lover, spoke first to Skip without acknowledging Esposito who opened the conversation.

"That was a dope head who lives down the way. She's fun talking to."

"That's probably the same thing she tells all her dope head friends," Cade said in an unprovoked slap. He knew he'd gone too far, so he quickly recovered by offering help. "How about Taco Bell later?" Cade said as he looked at the time display on his radio. He figured he may have to spring for Cracker Barrel or some other breakfast serving establishment. Esposito turned toward Uncle Frank's and picked up the pace. He rushed as if Taco Bell would be closing soon or the offer may be withdrawn.

"And bring your list of probation officers," Cade shouted. Esposito raised his hand without looking back to indicate he heard the request. Cade pulled alongside an abandoned car in what used to be Uncle Frank's front yard. The car seemed to be more decoration than a mode of transportation. Esposito burst out the door, letting it slam behind him. The door flung open again before Esposito was even off the porch. The senior Esposito stepped outside and launched a string of profanity directed at the "stunad." The *stunad* explained this was Italian slang for *jackass*.

"I'll bring you some lunch," Esposito yelled at his uncle, as Cade waved to the man standing in a T-shirt and boxers. Cade made a U-turn as he repeated the word *stunad* to himself in an effort to memorize it. The term would certainly come in handy in the future.

Cade pulled into the empty Taco Bell parking lot with a clear view of the two employees inside. They were preparing for the day. With a hint of excitement in his voice, Esposito began explaining the notations in his "legal book." Cade hadn't even noticed the book in Esposito's lap. The book was a black and white marble-looking composition book. It reminded Cade of the nervous excitement surrounding the week or so before school starting back. The time when kids crowd in the stationery aisle at Wal-Mart, searching for the perfect three-ring binders and the latest backpack fashion.

Cade sometimes thought his investigative work mirrored his old school habits. He always started with a burst of excitement, but then he resorted to mediocre effort and sloppy paperwork once the newness wore off. Even the Doctor LNU case was getting old. This staleness was seen in the number of other investigators volunteering to assist in the investigation.

Cade listened to Esposito who began telling his side of the long list of arrests. He listened while watching one of the two Taco Bell employees return to the prep line after taking out the morning trash. Cade began to wonder where the next closest Taco Bell was located after he observed the man return to food prep seconds after closing the rear door.

As if he was waiting on Cade's full attention before beginning his book review, Esposito attempted to make small talk.

"Whatcha think about that doctor killing dudes in the hood, man. That's some scary, nasty stuff." Cade didn't look away from the side windows of Taco Bell, but he stopped chewing sunflower seeds for a full second. "Are you kidding me?" Esposito said, with too much excitement and volume. Cade was impressed with the sharpness of the ex-drug user's mind. "It's your case?

Aw, man, I shoulda known!"

With two more cars now in the parking lot and the fine observation made by Esposito, Cade started the car and headed west down Highway 78. Esposito didn't speak until he saw which direction Cade was taking them.

"Am I about to witness that stupid thing government people say? You know, like, now that I know you're working the doctor killer case, you're gonna have to kill me?"

Cade hit his right turn signal at the old Hardees. It had been turned into a third rate Chinese buffet years after the two men's high school graduation. Esposito realized they were two blocks from their Alma Mater.

"You takin' me back to school, Maddy?"

Cade was convinced he could use his speaking abilities to deliver a sound message to Esposito to start his rehabilitation.

"We had good times here, right?"

"Yep," Esposito answered, now more somber as he saw the school had been closed. "I haven't been here since the day we graduated," Esposito said in nearly a whisper. Cade pointed to the first row of broken windows.

"Remember climbing out Mr. Fikes' room and ripping your jacket?"

"Yeah," Esposito said with a fond smile. "My mom threw it out a while back 'cause it was ripped. You believe that? My dang letterman jacket, man."

Unlike the way he typically spoke, Cade paused to prepare his next few comments.

"You know the average person looking at this place would think it was a piece of crap school," Cade said as he drove over pylons which were intended to keep out intruders. "I mean, even people who lived next door may have thought this place was a dump. But we know differently because we have so many memories here." He was afraid to pause in the conversation in fear that Esposito would insert some humor, and he'd lose the moment.

"This place is old and worn down, Ang. A few years ago, the land owner filed bankruptcy and gave up on selling it. It's just sitting here rotting because it's hard to find tucked away back here. Nobody has even taken the time to see the potential like we know because we can picture Mr. Faught and Ms. Crabtree. Even Fikes and that goofball Woods gave us some good laughs."

Esposito stared at the glove compartment, and Cade felt like he may have hit home. Esposito's somber look made it appear as though he understood the analogy between a broken and abandoned school and a broken and abandoned ex-high school superstar.

"'Recon Fikes' daughter is still hot?" Esposito asked, with a serious level of interest. Cade felt the rejection of his first try and turned his focus on finding an out-of-sight parking spot behind the old school. He finally stopped the car and adjusted the radio for just the right mood music. He began a second effort at a serious conversation.

His pause gave Esposito the time to soak in the school's conditions. Esposito had focused in on the press box resting above the top row of bleachers. The announcers' box somehow looked more maintained than the school itself. Esposito was twenty feet from the SUV by the time Cade could follow.

Cade trailed behind as Esposito climbed the concrete steps of the home side of Seminole Field. Sitting down directly under the announcer's box, Esposito spoke in an even quieter voice.

"This is where my dad used to sit. Right here so he could stand up and give Old Man Woods a piece of his mind when he called the wrong numbers."

When Esposito mentioned his dad, Cade found himself at a loss of words. Esposito looked out across the field he commanded two decades ago. He fiddled with a toothpick that seemed to appear from thin air.

"That was the first time I tried crack; when I came home for the funeral. I had everything, and touched that garbage to my lips just one time, and I was hooked." Esposito did not care that Cade saw him cry. It was clear to Cade that Esposito had no concern about vulnerabilities or weakness. His defenses and his pride were quickly fading.

For the first time in Cade's adulthood, he didn't feel like he could fix a problem with his gift of gab. He sat down by his old friend and stared out at an imaginary game played during a time when the two had far less worries.

Cade looked at the display on his cell phone and realized they had been sitting on the unforgiving concrete for nearly an hour. About to suggest they revisit Taco Bell, Cade stopped short as Esposito pulled the marble notebook from his back pocket.

The notebook was bent and crammed with torn pieces of index cards, wrinkled and wet paper, and notes written in various colors. One in particular stood out. It was a napkin with a telephone number written in what appeared to be lipstick. Cade grabbed it for closer inspection. Esposito snatched it and stuck it in his back pocket.

Esposito turned to the cardboard backing of the notebook to show a half organized list of names and numbers. Cade's eyebrows rose slightly higher with every entry. Between and around the scribbled dates and dollar amounts, the list seemed to be referencing eight different probation officers.

"Ang," Cade said, almost at a whisper. He softly began speaking to Esposito in the same tone he used with his thirteen year-old daughter when he was attempting to get information without raising his voice and showing his frustration. "Does this mean you have probation cases with eight different police departments?"

"Nine," the defendant said, as he reached over to point out one of the names. "This dude right here handles Adamsville and Graysville both." Esposito was now holding a half-eaten apple which seemed to appear from the same place as the toothpick. The apple dripped a new stain on the long list of police and probation officers. Cade's brain went into a fight or flight mode. Either stick it out with Esposito or run like a mad man, he thought.

Halfway through the list, Cade stopped on the entry of *Grandy, Helena Police, DNL.* Cade recognized the *DNL* as *driving with no license,* and he recognized Grandy as a guy who owed him a favor.

After Cade's father suffered his second heart attack three years prior, he had become motivated to hit the gym. After passing on a couple of gyms filled with muscle-head steroid freaks, he found a family oriented all night facility close to home that allowed 24/7 access. During the sign up process, because of the twelve month contract, Cade provided his true name and almost true place of employment to the gym manager, a man who obviously was no stranger to steroids himself. Cade overlooked the probable drug usage, hoping it was in the past, based on the gym's family feel.

The meaty manager quickly admitted to Cade that he'd spent his entire childhood and most of his adult life wishing he would have gotten into law enforcement. He added that an assault, brought on by the cliché *roid rage,* ended his childhood dream and kept him doing the only thing he knew, working out. Cade remained off duty, and didn't question the man further. But Grandy pressed on, giving all the unwanted details of the late-night brawl, instigated by a jealous man of course, which got him twelve months in prison.

He remembered Grandy sliding the contract across the gym counter for review. The triplicate form reflected twelve months of personal training, billed at $50 an hour, with a line through the price and "KG" scribbled in its place. Grandy smiled and said he'd gladly give up the fee to hear war stories of a life he'd dreamed about. Within six months, Cade had gained eighteen pounds of muscle and told more made up stories than he could remember.

During the next six months, the investigator began investigating a little, and learned that although Grandy had initially been charged with a felony assault, he pled guilty to a single misdemeanor harassment charge, and therefore was not barred from law enforcement as he'd been erroneously informed. Within another six months, Grandy was the newest Helena street cop. After only half that time, his muscles, constantly challenging the poorly made polyester uniform, got him noticed and moved into the narcotics unit, where he vowed to never leave. The move cost Cade the near-daily company of a good friend, and at least ten pounds added to his now squishy midsection.

Cade's mental picture turned off one old inmate to refocus on the other one.

"How'd you lose your license?" Esposito paused as if he didn't hear the question. He carefully aimed the apple core at a rusty garbage can left along the sideline for some reason, as many as twenty years ago. He missed by five feet.

"It was after the robbery," Esposito said, as if everyone knew about the robbery.

"Robbery!"

"Look, Mad, one day I'll tell you the whole deal. It's all gonna be in the book, man. But that Helena thing is the stupidest. I was driving to clean out a guy's gutters for fifty bucks and got profiled cause of my long hair and the beat up car I was driving."

"I don't think stupidest is a word," Cade said, as he flipped open his cell phone and began thumbing through his contacts. With his thumb on the send button, Cade said, "You want to do some work right now?"

"What kind of work?" Esposito asked. Cade just looked at him as if to say beggars can't be choosers. "Yeah, man, anything."

"Ang," Cade continued, changing topics and tone. His thumb was still resting on the send button. "How do you know about the case, the *doctor* case?"

"I read the paper every day, man. Plus, most of the people I see on a regular basis have a real interest in the matter." Cade wondered if he meant cops or drug users, or both. He felt like he had just used some prejudiced rationalization in assuming a man with little money would read the paper.

"I guess I figured a man with no cell phone funds wouldn't have newspaper funds either."

"Well, you know, cell phones and newspapers are two different things. My neighbor's cell phone doesn't get delivered every day in a nice plastic bag just twenty feet from Uncle Frank's porch."

"I'm calling the police." Cade pressed the send button as he laughed at the theft confession.

CHAPTER 12

Esposito listened to the one-sided conversation as if he was trying to tune out static of a radio station to hear some breaking news event. Cade had to walk down to the lower aisle and around to the old concession stand for decent cell coverage.

Cade felt sure Grandy and Esposito could work out some arrangement whereby Esposito would bring someone more desirable to the attention of the police department. He hoped that if Esposito could assist the department, they would be so grateful they may permanently postpone Esposito's legal battle. There would always be other criminals to take Esposito's place.

Cade planned to simply make introductions then bow out because he wasn't quite sure how to make his relationship with Esposito seem official.

"M-C!" was how Grandy answered, and Cade was pleased that his number must not have been deleted from Grandy's contacts. He was surprised to learn that

Grandy was free for the afternoon because one *client*, a would-be arrestee, got arrested by another department earlier in the day.

Before Cade committed to drive Esposito to Helena, he turned to him to get some reassurance that Esposito was up for the meeting. Even though he didn't stay in close contact with Grandy, he still considered him a friend and certainly didn't want Esposito embarrassing him. Angelo was suddenly missing in action, and Cade found himself standing alone.

"I'll call you right back, man," Cade said. He ended the call before even determining if Grandy or any of his colleagues were interested.

Cade rounded the stadium steps to see Esposito standing at midfield, crouched in his under-center quarterback position. Esposito called out a play as he looked out over both sides of his offensive line. Cade leaned against the rusty fence, soaking in the nostalgia. Esposito stepped back in the pocket and delivered a perfect imaginary forty yard pass to his imaginary tight end for another school victory.

Esposito seemed a little embarrassed when he realized Cade was watching the detailed reenactment of some past game. Esposito jogged off the field to hear the plan.

"Nice pass, man," Cade said. Esposito picked up speed. The quarterback put his shoulder into Cade's midsection with just enough energy to quickly pick him up in the fireman's carry position. Esposito acted as if he wasn't already carrying around the weight of the world. After being gently dropped back to earth, Cade relayed possible plans for a meeting with Helena detectives on step number one of wiping out past debt.

The short drive to Helena was a quiet one. After a follow-up call to Grandy confirming the visit, Cade focused on the cases he should be working. The SUV was quiet. It was unclear to Cade if Esposito was or could focus on anything at all.

Cade pulled around back of the Helena Police Department to a gaggle of officers standing outside the prisoner intake sallyport.

"A freakin' sallyport," Esposito said, sounding like the city's finance manager. Cade knew he was curious how such a small town justified the spending on a feature usually reserved for larger agencies. Cade also found it a little disheartening that his friend knew the word *sallyport*, a word typically only used by law enforcement or those who were regularly processed through one.

Cade parked with the passenger side closest to the officers, which made them a little uneasy until Grandy informed the group that Cade was bringing a "snitch" to see what he knew about some locals. All but one officer, the newest on the force, visibly relaxed.

Esposito watched with a tinge of jealousy as Cade shook hands with the officers and joked with a couple. He was particularly interested in the attractive female officer. He finally exited the passenger side just as she turned to reenter the department. Esposito waited to speak until his feminine target had one hand on the front door.

"Miss, could you point me to the restroom?" Because Cade had seen Esposito urinating on the visitor side of Seminole Field just a half an hour before, he knew Esposito was creating a reason to speak with the detective. That was one thing, at least, that hadn't changed much since high school. Esposito wouldn't miss an opportunity to flirt with a good-looking woman regardless of his situation. Cade tried to dismiss the effort but kept an eye on his responsibility through the tinted windows of the police department lobby.

After some one-liner, Esposito was apparently shot down. Cade was relieved to see Esposito and the attractive officer part ways. Cade made a mental note to find out which line Esposito attempted to use with the attractive police detective whom he knew as Detective Tina Whitley.

When the sergeant extinguished his cigarette, the other three narcotics officers, including Detective Grandy, followed his lead and spit their tobacco into the neatly trimmed bushes lining the rear entrance of the department. They all followed their boss into the squad room for a chat with the potential new informant. After the introductions, Cade told the sergeant and his sloppily dressed narcotics officers he'd wait in the lobby. He tried not to focus on the fact that he had just transported a friend to a police department to arrange work in which he shared no jurisdiction.

Cade justified his actions by thinking he'd recruit Esposito as an informant himself at some point. Cade decided he could articulate that it was appropriate to work with informants to help them resolve any personal issues which may interfere with their ability to support a federal investigation.

Cade knew his anal retentive boss wouldn't see it his way. But then again, he seldom did see things Cade's way. The mental picture of his fifty something year-old boss was replaced by the real image of the fifty something year-old police lieutenant.

"Agent Cade, what would you like for us to do with your man?" Cade didn't like the sound of any of that. Not the *Agent Cade* formality, not the request for guidance, and certainly not the direct connection with a man still standing at a fork in the road leading to drug addiction or normalcy. He decided to ignore the implications and move on with business.

"I'm working with the guy on a case, and when I found out he has tickets here, I thought I'd bring him by to see if he could be of use to you. If he is, maybe y'all can help each other, and I'll have him available to do my dirty work if he's not visiting with probation officers once a week."

Cade was truly a master of the hidden message. In Cade's mind, the, "I'm working with the guy" statement wasn't untrue even though he knew the lieutenant would believe it to mean Esposito was deeply involved in a federal investigation. The phrase, "could be of use to you" was used to stroke the proud manager's ego by suggesting a human life was like a tool or a gadget for the use and disposal by a powerful officer of the law like him. And the phrase, "do my dirty work" was intended to bring the lieutenant back from ego atmosphere by understanding Cade's position was one of power as well.

The look in the lieutenant's eyes was a trophy to Cade. He realized he'd found the mark on all accounts. It was just another human interaction that subconsciously strengthened Cade's thoughts that he would one day finish that book on effective communication.

Cade and the lieutenant knocked on the interrogation room door and entered to see Esposito and two of the three drug agents pointing at photos of some of Helena's finest residents.

"This guy moved to Alabaster. He's living with a meth head named Lucy." The identification was noted by the two officers.

"Can you buy from him?" Grandy asked.

Esposito was sharp and on full alert like a shortstop ready for anything hit his way. He enjoyed believing he was part of the police team, although he was only a weapon for the narcotics unit until his information dried up. Everyone in the room, except Esposito, knew it.

"You can't buy from him 'cause he don't have anything. He gets everything he has from Lucy, and she's mad at me right now." Cade was disturbed a bit after looking at the photo of Lucy which the lieutenant pulled up from the photo database. He was glad Esposito didn't offer information on what set off Lucy. He didn't want to know.

Cade realized the officers must have been planning to arrest Grandy's target because they all seemingly had the time and energy to work with Esposito to find just the right replacement. The lieutenant held a photo of a typical meth user. The mug shot looked as though Lucy was dragged out of bed at 2 a.m. for the photo. Esposito continued flipping pages of the photo album filled with driver's license photos.

"Catfish!" Esposito's excited announcement turned all five heads in the room.

"This guy is Catfish?"

"Don't he look like a catfish?" Esposito shot back.

Not more than twenty minutes later, Esposito and Cade pulled into the only undesirable section of the growing town of Helena in a police seized 1998 Mercury. Cade sat in the passenger seat with his hat pulled low and slightly cocked to one side.

Cade's upper middle class lifestyle didn't allow him the natural undercover look of long hair or a thug-like appearance. But both men knew it was not out of the ordinary for a drug buyer to bring a lookout. They also knew it was against drug buying rules for an unknown individual to talk or interact with the sellers unless they indicated a need or desire to check him out.

The nervous excitement quickly gave way to

boredom as the two sat quietly in Catfish's unpaved driveway. Even the Rottweiler chained to an old tree by the back shed got tired of barking at the two intruders after a while.

Even though it did certainly qualify as boring, it was still Cade's favorite part of the job. He tried to describe it at every school career day when the kids asked this standby question. His response was always to describe this moment, when his heart beat fast and his mind raced through a hundred scenarios of what could happen. Usually, none of them did, but it was a rush none the less. This was what he assumed was the fascination with bass fishing; the anticipation and possibilities of catching a big one. Cade figured his anticipation towered above that of a fisherman because fishermen didn't usually have a chance of getting killed while waiting to land the largemouth bass.

He drifted off to a moment in his childhood when he was forced out of bed at five in the morning after telling his dad the night before that he wanted to go out on the next early morning expedition. The cold air in the boat would force the young Maddy awake as he hunkered down under the seats to stay warm. He could clearly see the images of his uncles Pinky and Bob, moving like a team but arguing like an old married couple.

Esposito was the first to break the silence, bringing Cade back from his uncles fighting over the last minnow and deciding finally to bite it in half.

"Any pointers, Mr. BS Artist?" Cade did not move.

"You know, Ang, I have traveled all across the country teaching people how to deal with other people: bankers, government folks, teachers, cops. But I don't think there's anything I can teach you about shoveling manure." Esposito looked over at Cade as if the two were on a date.

"You always were a good talker, Mad. Maybe we should team up to write my book. I can add an *s* to the end of the title." Cade didn't respond. Esposito slowly called out variations of his new book title as if making a final decision. "The Hustlers. The Hust-lers. The Mighty Hustlers." Cade was amused with Esposito's passion.

"Actually, Ang, I am working on a book. Probably not as exciting as yours. I mean, I've never been a stripper."

"Male dancer," Esposito responded, in a serious effort to enlighten Cade on the correct terminology of adult male reviews. "What's it called?" he asked as Cade looked in his direction without lifting his head from the tattered headrest.

"What? Male dancing?"

"No, man. The book you're gonna put out. What's it called and how you gonna fit me in?"

With only slight hesitation because he hadn't even told Kelly he was seriously trying to write a book, Cade heard the title of his fantasized book stated out loud.

It's called, "Search and Seizure of Opportunities for Effectiveness," Cade said, with just the right delivery.

"When's it coming out?" Esposito seriously asked, and Cade realized Esposito had never taken one serious step toward writing a book, or he'd know it just wasn't that easy.

"Well, since I started writing it about five years ago, I'd..."

"Five years? How long is it?" Cade looked back at the target house and focused on his day job. Deep down, he knew being a writer and speaker was just a pipe dream. He resorted to sarcasm to end the conversation.

"Longer than yours."

A few minutes passed. The two stared into the oncoming sunset waiting on Catfish to come home from who knows where. Almost in a whisper, Esposito pushed again for more information.

"So, really, what's it about?" Cade hesitated at first but realized that even talking to a recovering drug addict was a good first step at sharing his written work with some other human. Cade repositioned in his seat as he thought, for the first time ever, about how to describe his five years of writing to even a single person audience.

"The book is made up of interview tactics that have worked over the years in dealing with people in undesirable situations." Esposito would make it hard for Cade to stay on target.

"So there's a lot in there about buying burritos for people?" Cade folded his arms in protest and looked out the dirty window again at Catfish's uneven front stoop. "Alright, seriously, go on. Tactics like what?" Cade adjusted his hat as if allowing for more organized thought.

"For example, some of my cases, like the Doctor LNU, are freakin' complicated puzzles. While I'm a decent investigator, I'm pretty unorthodox." Cade knew Esposito must be thinking of a dozen comments, and he was surprised Esposito refrained from continued interruption.

"Over the years, when I've had to work with other cops, I tried to team up with people I liked. The days are long sometimes, you know. I hate sitting in a car all day with some goofball. The problem I had was that usually, to help pass the time, I picked people I got along with. Over time, I realized I liked these people because we shared the same thoughts and ideas. So really, I never helped my situation because these people usually agreed with every stupid idea I had. They agreed because they had the same stupid thoughts. That's why I chose them in the first place." Esposito squinted his eyes, and Cade knew he was trying to follow along.

"So what's the tactic, avoid stupid thinking people?" Esposito asked with actual commitment. Cade chose his words carefully before continuing. He saw a glimpse of an opportunity to continue the rehabilitation. Maybe Esposito would climb out of that pit after all.

"The tactics come in pairs. There's a minimum and a maximum. It's different from most self-help books which are garbage."

"Except that Chicken Soup book, man. That's a

good read. Or at least it was in jail with nothing better to do."

"Other than jailed inmates, most people pick up a self-help book 'cause they are struggling with some issue in their life. They read a book and think they can wake up one day carrying on like Doctor Phil or some other tree hugging moron and be a different person. Truth is, a person who has been a jerk for years can't just read a book and stop being a jerk. They just can't. These methods give boundaries so you don't have to be a totally different person overnight, just modify a bit."

The passion in Cade's voice told Esposito to just sit and soak it in. At least he pretended to soak it in. Cade pressed on. "So, for example, this tactic or method is *surround yourself with effective people,* and part B of the tactic is *don't confuse likable people with effective people.* And the point is that sometimes you actually work as a better team with someone you don't see eye to eye with because…"

The book report was interrupted by a horrible crashing noise.

CHAPTER 13

Cade and Esposito both felt the violent downward jarring of the rear of the old Mercury. Cade's heart was beating in his throat. The would-be drug buyers quickly turned to see the outline of a large man.

The shadow of a man, presumed to be Catfish, was standing on the trunk of the car. Even in the midst of possible danger, Cade took a few seconds to think about his stupidity in allowing this threat to sneak up on the two of them. He hoped Grandy and the others were trained well enough to sit tight and not move in on the action.

Cade felt for the butt of his semi-automatic, but kept his hands away from the door handle. Esposito, not trained in these situations, allowed his instincts to take over as he forcefully opened the door to face the threat. Catfish jumped off the car to the gravel below and recognized Esposito somewhere in midair.

After an unusual but quick rekindling of some old drug seller/buyer relationship, the two walked, almost embracing, up the driveway to Catfish's front porch. Cade wondered if Catfish even knew he was there.

Cade sat silently and watched as Catfish felt Esposito from his shoulders to lower back. He figured Esposito's adrenalin would not allow him to feel what the trained undercover agent had to assume was a decent pat down for a recorder. *Oh Crap, the recorder!* Cade realized too late that the body wire which had been left off to conserve battery was still off as Esposito now stood arm in arm with the catch of the day.

Without too much thought, Cade unholstered his semi-automatic and transferred the weapon to his left hand. He firmly grasped the old door handle. With little time to formulate a plan, he took a breath and opened the door. The pop of the seldom used passenger door hinge made Esposito and Catfish turn toward the third wheel. Cade held his gun low, pressed against his leg and in the shadows, out of sight from Catfish. Catfish held a gun of his own.

Cade tried to control his breathing as Catfish raised what appeared to be a .38 revolver. He pointed the weapon directly at Cade who knew he could not bring his pistol on target quickly enough to surprise Catfish. Instead, he dropped the weapon onto the passenger seat. The worn out springs allowed for a soft and silent fall. Cade abandoned his role as a shooter for that of an actor.

"Hey, man, take it easy," Cade said in a voice that was his best guess at how a man sounded when he was stoned. "The stunad there needs my money, bro." Esposito put his hands on Catfish's weapon which was tilted at an angle that would make one think he was filming a video for MTV. He whispered something in the ear of his seller as he pushed the threat slowly back to Catfish's side. Catfish chuckled at what Cade figured was some off color comment.

Catfish continued laughing as he slid the gun back in the waistband of his pants. Esposito turned his back to Catfish and walked to within six inches of Cade. Cade spoke some incoherent words loud enough for his voice to carry to the target. He simultaneously reached directly forward, ensuring his actions were concealed from Catfish by Esposito's thin frame. He put two fingers just inside the front of Esposito's denim shorts.

"Mad," Esposito whispered, "don't get me excited, man. I'm about to buy drugs." Cade quickly found the small on/off switch and felt it move from the *off* to the *on* position.

Cade pulled a ten dollar bill from his pocket and stuffed it in Esposito's hand, hoping he would remember he had fifty dollars, taken from Helena's buy fund, in his back pocket. Esposito returned to Catfish and the two entered the old trailer without looking back.

As was generally expected with police surveillance equipment, the outdated transmitter in Esposito's pants transmitted more static than words. After a few frustrating seconds, Cade lowered the window an inch or so in an effort to hear anything unfiltered by the thin walls of the mobile home. Nothing.

The front door flew open as quickly as it had been closed. Esposito emerged with a smile and a clinched hand which no doubt would hold the prize of a few pills or a small amount of crack. He was talking about his target before he could get the door closed. Cade put his finger to his lips, giving the *shh* sign as he pointed to Esposito's crotch, reminding his new quasi partner that he was still recording.

After leaving the long and uneven gravel driveway, and with the recorder safely in Cade's lap and in the off position, Esposito began beaming like a school girl who'd just been asked to the prom.

"I was made for this stuff, Mad. And I could help you with that book." Cade was surprised to hear Esposito return to the conversation that Catfish interrupted. "Just there, inside, I saw four guns, not counting the one you met. There was at least six ounces of coke on the kitchen table. I was alone, Mad, but unlike you, I always work alone. No one will work with me. People don't even see me, Maddy. I don't have the benefit of surrounding myself with anybody I want. I have to take what I can. I knew Catfish wanted me to do a line in there. He had a gun at my head, Mad."

The massive change in adrenalin levels seemed to hit Esposito, and he appeared, only now, to consider the extreme danger he'd faced. Esposito paused to allow the fear to catch up with his brain. Cade had now experienced two failures within an hour.

"What'd you do?" Cade asked, with remorse for putting his friend in such danger. Esposito pulled into the police parking lot next to the team of officers already discussing the logistics of a search warrant.

"I used what I had. Catfish's girlfriend was passed out on the couch. I flirted with her like there was no tomorrow. Even put my hands on her big ol' bubble butt."

"In front of her man?" Cade asked, clearly surprised. Esposito looked over at Cade with a look of victory on his face.

"Yeah, 'cause only a stoned idiot would hit on Catfish's girlfriend with Catfish holding a gun. That convinced him I was wasted, and he just told me to go home." Cade was reminded that Esposito, too, possessed a remarkable gift of gab.

"Listen, Maddy, I don't mean to trash the book. People who shop at Barnes and Noble with espresso drinks buy that sort of stuff, but it just ain't real, Mad." After a long pause, Esposito added, "No offense, man. I mean it'll sell, just not to my people." Cade promised himself to give up on the book once and for all. Esposito was right and maybe the only one in the world who would have been so honest.

Esposito handed over the keys to the beat up Mercury to the first officer he saw when he climbed out of the car.

"It feels good driving illegally while a bunch of cops watch and don't pull you over." Pleased with their new drug buyer, the comment received a chuckle from the police audience. Esposito seemed to be as happy as Cade ever remembered seeing him, even throughout their school days twenty years earlier. Cade knew the officers would hit the trailer in less than twenty-four hours with a search warrant. He planned to be nowhere near. He wrapped the long antenna of the body wire around the recorder. He handed the listening equipment to the pleased lieutenant who spoke to Cade loud enough for Esposito to hear.

"You guys did good. Good buy. Let's go make copies of everything and get it into evidence. We'll need to search you, too, Angelo," he said nodding to Grandy. Esposito immediately spread eagle against the hood of the nearest vehicle without apparent insult. Grandy did a quick and less than diligent pat down, which seemed to be a message that he trusted Esposito and was just following orders. It reminded Cade how much he liked Grandy's style.

"Send me the ticket numbers too, and we'll see what we can do," the lieutenant said, already halfway back inside his department.

Cade hit the door release button on his SUV and Esposito jumped back into his more comfortable role as a passenger. Cade glanced in the rearview mirror to ensure he didn't scrape one of the brightly painted blue marked cars. He spotted Officer Whitley and wondered to himself how she managed to avoid the undercover buy and surveillance.

Cade turned on the radio as he would for his kids to keep them entertained. He opened the door before Esposito could ask where he was going.

"Just a second," he said, as the door was closing behind him. Esposito tuned in the Howard Stern radio show while watching Cade through the repositioned rearview mirror. He eyed Cade speaking to someone inside the station lobby. As Cade opened the door to step inside, she came into focus. Esposito saw Cade hug the woman Catfish made him forget for only a brief time. More importantly, Esposito saw Whitley hug Cade back!

Cade returned to the car, jumped behind the wheel, and threw the vehicle in reverse.

"It's getting late, man. You up for a little Taco Bell?" Esposito didn't need to answer, because he hadn't turned down Taco Bell in six consecutive offers. Cade drove west into the sunset over I-65. Esposito rehashed the drug buy a dozen different ways, explaining the events in great detail. Cade knew all versions were colorfully embellished.

At some point in Esposito's story, Cade began organizing his plans for the next day. He felt as if he had lost momentum with Esposito by spending the day playing cops and drug dealers in a case he had no business being a part of.

Cade's lack of participation in the conversation allowed for a long pause when Esposito finished his fifth or sixth version of the near death experience. Cade realized Esposito had stopped talking and glanced at him, thinking he may have fallen asleep. Esposito was staring at Cade in a way that begged for him to explain something.

"What? Are you waiting on me to say you did good? You did good, man." Esposito didn't speak for a few seconds, as if he was trying to use the awkward silence to create suspense.

"Are you sleeping with my girlfriend?"

"Which one?" Cade said, in an obvious dodge. He figured Esposito had to know the reply was a stall tactic.

"My how the tables have turned. Now look at the great Maddison Cade, stalling for an answer, while I, the untrained interviewer, have you by the short hair. What's going on with you and Officer Hot Pants, Mad?" He had Cade on the ropes.

"Wait!" Esposito shouted, maintaining control of the conversation. "Let me use one of your tactics. Here's a little evidence to think about before you lie, 'cause if you lie, you won't be able to reverse your position due to your enormous ego. That's what you've taught me, right?" Cade stared through the windshield as if he was driving in a hard rain.

"We pulled up to the police department, and you shook hands like you were at the United Nations. You didn't talk to my girlfriend as far as I could tell, but later, you left with a hug and kiss on the cheek. So did your relationship progress from a stiff handshake to a kiss in less than two hours with no conversation?

Maybe you already had a relationship, huh? And if so, why'd you hide that relationship from me and my new buddies unless there's something to hide?"

Esposito dragged out that question like a prosecuting attorney's cross examination before a group of jurors who were hanging on every word. Cade lifted his turn signal, so Esposito filled the quiet space.

"You pullin' over to shoot me? Don't want to bloody the interior?"

"No, I just thought Jim 'N Nick's would be a treat for you since you didn't embarrass me tonight."

"You mean a treat or a bribe?" Esposito shot back, but Cade refused to be shaken. Verbally dueling with Esposito was a good feeling. Both men were in places in their lives where they could use a few more friends to horse around with. The SUV came to a stop in a space around back and both men seemed content to sit, wasting precious barbeque time, enjoying a feeling of camaraderie that neither had felt in a long time.

Esposito adjusted the satellite radio and found very appropriate eighties music. Cade began an attempt at a serious conversation just as Prince and the Revolution started belting out *Kiss*. Cade paused, thinking Esposito may have travelled back mentally to a better time in his life. Esposito looked out the window and quietly began impersonating Prince's falsetto, "Gotta not talk dirty baby, if you wanna impress me." He stopped when he felt Cade's eyes on him, and started speaking as if in mid-conversation.

"It's like the whole world is against me, man."

"All the more reason to pull your crap together and prove everybody wrong," Cade shot back, jumping into the seriousness of the new topic.

"You don't get it, Mad! You're talking about stuff you've never been involved with?"

"I see it every day, Ang. Dopers screwing up their lives and the lives of anybody stupid enough to get close to them." The tone of the conversation had escalated quickly. Esposito turned to face Cade with his jaws clinched. He brought the volume back to normal.

"Is that what I did? I screwed up everybody's life? Well you certainly don't want that, Special Agent Perfect Life, cause deep down, you know you're just here for you, your case, your conscience and your reputation for charity work. I don't need your help and I don't need you!" He had returned to the previous level of yelling and then some. Esposito slid from the SUV and slammed the door behind him, walking through the restaurant's parking lot toward Highway 280, some twenty miles from his home. Cade caught up with him near the restaurant's overflowing dumpster.

"What do you need, crack head? You need a hit?" Cade kept his eyes tilted slightly upward into Esposito's while digging in his pockets for money. "Here's twenty bucks to add to the ten you were planning on stealing from me. Will that buy a decent rock? Like you said, I don't know much about drug buying." He had intended on pressing the bill against Esposito's chest, but due to his level of frustration, it ended up more like a punch. Esposito knocked Cade's arm away and the twenty dollar bill fell gently to the concrete.

Esposito, feeling his back against the wall, or dumpster to be more literal, returned the aggression with a shove that caught Cade off guard and off balance. He struggled to keep his feet, embarrassed that maybe a drug addict was strong enough to hold his own against the trained agent. Cade only briefly considered going one on one with Esposito before drawing his weapon and bringing it in line with Esposito's right eye.

"How 'bout this? Is this better? You could shoot up, but let's just get it over with. Maybe we put your mother out of her misery."

"Do it, you jackass!" Esposito whispered. Cade stayed on target for only a few seconds before lowering the weapon. He grabbed the barrel of the dark steel with his left hand, and rotated it to his right. He held it out to Esposito, the muzzle now facing his own chest.

"Take it and do it yourself." Esposito took the weapon, surprising Cade just a little, and immediately pulled back the hammer. He pressed the nose of the gun into the firm underside of his chin. His eyes widened as if he was giving himself a countdown. Cade's brain went into overdrive, trying to decide if he should quickly reach for the gun or allow the scene to play out, praying he'd not go to jail himself if Esposito pulled the trigger.

Esposito's index finger moved from trigger guard to trigger, and Cade knew the slightest flinch would cause

Esposito's life and his own career to be killed simultaneously. The hammer fell with a heavy thud that sounded as loud as the shot that did not go off. Esposito had chosen to press the trigger release instead of the trigger, making the weapon safe as the hammer fell against the safety mechanism.

Esposito dropped the gun and slid down the side of the dumpster to the food-covered concrete below. Cade, realizing the significance of this moment for both men, recovered his weapon and sat beside Esposito who was now crying. Cade, too, was on the verge of tears, but didn't know if it was the fear of a near catastrophic event or the replaying of Esposito's accusations that may have just proven to be true.

In a split second, it occurred to Cade that in this true life-or-death scenario, his mind instinctively rested on the issue of self-preservation. He might have been less concerned about the death of a man than the death of his career. He realized Esposito had been right about him. Perhaps he did only care about himself.

Nearly five minutes passed without a word, and not one passerby even noticed the two. Both men stared at the back of Jim 'N Nick's which had a huge flying pig racing toward the moon. They appeared to be looking through the restaurant, maybe at a mental highlight film showing mistakes they'd made in life.

Esposito broke the silence with an apology which was quickly returned by Cade. They volleyed excuses back and forth a few more rounds before the conversation returned to inappropriate discussion about Tina Whitley, Mr. Fikes' daughter and a few other classmates they'd chased on the once prestigious fields and hallways of West Birmingham Christian.

Kelly's turn to be discussed came around, and Esposito reminded Cade how lucky he was to have the American dream of a beautiful wife and two kids tucked safely away in the suburbs. Cade didn't need to respond. It was obvious he had a wonderful life and it was painfully obvious that Esposito, while saying it out of frustration, had spoken the truth about his level of selfishness.

"I'll tell you all about your girlfriend over some cheese biscuits."

CHAPTER 14

To Cade, Jim 'N Nick's was the best barbeque in Birmingham, if not the whole free world. At 8 p.m., the place was packed. Over his usual Pig in the Garden Salad, Cade shared his side of his second heartbreak since ninth grade.

Cade and Whitley were both clerks in a large agency filled with ladder climbers and egomaniacs. The two were hard workers and were both chasing their own dreams of making it in the government. Although Cade and Kelly had dated for a while, they were in their *dating other people* stage. When Kelly began college, her experiences in sorority life were too much for the slightly jealous Cade. He thought being without her was better than being with her but on the outside of her college friends.

Whitley dreamed of settling down with a man and 2.5 kids. Cade, fresh out of a serious relationship, was thinking more about traveling the world for truth and justice before bringing kids into the mix. Esposito hung on every word like a romance novel as Cade shared what he had with no one else.

"After a ten hour day, in the parking garage on a Friday afternoon, I heard myself tell her I love her. It was like an out-of-body experience." Cade recalled how he looked into Whitley's eyes, waiting on her reciprocating response, which did not come. "I was so upset I went to the local Navy recruiter the next morning and joined the Reserve program. I told everybody at the office I needed to add the experience to my resume. It was really just a way to get away from Whitley and everybody else who would eventually find out I got trampled in the parking garage."

The failed romance story was interrupted by the delivery of cheese biscuits by an attractive waitress who introduced herself as Monica. Cade felt a bit uncomfortable when he realized the woman was staring at his dinner date. Esposito's long, tangled hair and the sores on his face signaled some sort of sickness. He was reminded of who (or what) his old friend had become. After hearing the orders, Monica rushed off to the call of a table full of middle-aged golfers.

Acting as if he hadn't noticed the unspoken statement made by Monica, Esposito pushed for more.

"So how'd she get to the PD?"

"She and I both wanted to get out of the mailroom. She did it with the county, and I did it with the military which was kind of a stepping stone to the feds in Washington. I heard she got married, and Kelly and I got back together about the same time. We see each other every now and then. I think we both know we had real feelings for each other." Esposito, with a mouth full of his third biscuit, didn't let the conversation turn sappy.

"Please tell me you never made out with her. It'll blow it for me." Cade grinned and thought about embellishing a story of his own.

"No, we didn't. I think we both wanted to and had the chance, but both respected the other's marriage too much." Monica returned with the orders. Esposito, now deeply vested in the story, only grinned as she made the delivery and spun away to another table.

"Or maybe you knew Kelly would have castrated you, huh?"

"Yeah, that too. So a couple years ago, she made it from the jail to a detective slot at Helena. I probably look too hard for a good reason to get out there to see her." Esposito was well involved with his rib plate.

"So you never made out with her?" Esposito asked again, as if he was seriously trying to decide whether or not to pursue her. Cade laughed out loud at Esposito's persistence.

Esposito was dropped back at the safety of Mama Esposito's at nearly 11 p.m. Cade headed back home through the more upscale traffic filled Hwy 280. Georgia greeted him at the door with her slobber covered tennis ball. Not another noise was heard from the house. Cade made his way to the bedroom where Kelly and their son lay nearly perfectly perpendicular to each other. Cade was left with less than a foot of space in their king size bed.

He kissed his son on the forehead and watched Kelly sleep for a few seconds. He felt a bit guilty about the trip down memory lane, and the *what if* thoughts he shared with Esposito. He looked at his bride and the miniature version of himself sleeping beside her. He considered himself lucky for how it all turned out.

It would be another night of little sleep and lots of brain activity. He was eager to return to the search for a killer in the morning. He hoped Hartline was in his typical grumpy mood. After what seemed like only seconds of sleep, the Hartline show was ready to kick off.

Cade sat in the backseat of Hartline's SUV, well out of sight. The two agents agreed Hartline would go at it alone first. He knew Hartline was hoping to deal one-on-one with Snow without his verbosity or warm and fuzzy talk. He wondered if Snow would recognize the cliché of good cop/bad cop once he jumped in to save Snow from Hartline's reliable aggression. He wondered if Hartline would realize he'd been used.

As if he'd zoned out at some point in the commute to Snow's, Cade came to as Hartline opened the driver's door to face Snow. He was worried. He maneuvered in the back seat to peek through the bottom of the window. A low hanging tree limb blocked his view. He could not even recall the tree being there. He felt another wave of extreme concern. Things were out of his control. Things happening on Snow's porch and things inside his head and stomach seemed to be developing on their own.

He saw only glimpses of bodies but could tell Snow was off the porch and standing toe-to-toe with Hartline. His heart beat faster as Hartline approached the man. He listened with growing concern as the men started speaking in a tone that surprised even Cade. It seemed the fictitious stories told to Hartline may have been a bit much. Hartline was almost screaming at the man and a fight was sure to break out.

Cade made a quick decision to intervene before the fireworks began. It was like calling in a prizefighter and then canceling the fight before it started. But he knew he had no time for the reports required after an altercation.

He grabbed the door handle on the side of Hartline's SUV away from Snow. He hoped Snow would be so distracted he wouldn't notice Cade had been a passenger in his opponent's vehicle. He nearly dislocated his fingers as the locked handle snapped back in place. "Ahhhh!" Cade screamed. The backdoor handles had been disconnected for the purpose of criminal transport. He reached for his cell phone to send an urgent call to Hartline. The phone had slipped from his back pocket and was nowhere to be found. This was karma, Cade decided, for being so deceitful.

The sound of gunfire took one hundred percent of Cade's focus. "No! No! No!" he screamed even louder, as he jumped to the front seat to exit the vehicle. He could clearly see both men now. Hartline was still standing but was obviously held in place by the stiffness of his body caused by the shock of the bullet. Hartline's white MP5 Instructor shirt turned red in seconds. Cade felt sorrow, guilt and rage simultaneously. He also felt another disabled door handle. Snow approached with his gun outstretched. The shot to his shoulder was not as bad as anticipated.

He stood under the hot water in the shower for a full five minutes. He'd have to compliment Kelly later in the day about the power in her punch. He wondered what he was yelling in his sleep that caused her to wake him so violently.

He was packing the ground beans into the cappuccino maker when he heard the alarm he'd set for 6 a.m. He dreaded to call his firearms instructor and was thankful Hartline's voicemail picked up. He reluctantly left a message explaining the need to cancel yet another qualification day. Cade was back in the SUV less than six hours after parking it.

With less Hwy 280 traffic than usual, Cade managed to make it to Highway 78 well before 8 a.m. As he turned down Mr. Snow's drive, he could easily see the house was bare. The drug users, or maybe prostitutes Mr. Snow spoke so passionately about, most likely consumed the home within an hour of his departure. The Hartline scheme, and all the deception that went along with it, wasn't necessary after all. The house was obviously empty.

He pulled his baton from the middle console and tucked it in his waistband. He hoped not to use it, and he certainly didn't have the time for the paperwork a shooting would require. He wondered what kind of price Mr. Snow got for his inherited headache. He walked around the property asking himself why the whole time, but he just couldn't help himself. He had no other leads to chase.

The garbage can that had been his rock throwing target was in the middle of the backyard, overflowing with trash. The ground was covered with probably twice the amount of trash. The scene made him wonder why Snow didn't just throw the trash in the yard.

He stopped in his tracks and stared at the garbage. Within seconds, he had returned to his vehicle to deposit his baton that was no longer needed. He traded the weapon for a pair of latex gloves. Within another few seconds, Cade was emptying the garbage can, starting with two carryout containers of half eaten spaghetti, now being enjoyed by a healthy pool of maggots.

He was accustomed to seeing other people's trash, and certainly had the stomach for it. Once, during a search with the local police, he put a store-bought doughnut on the top of a target dumpster. After announcing a "wow," to several local police officers protecting his crime scene, he emerged from the dumpster holding the doughnut like a prize. The acting scored a few laughs until Cade bit into the find, forcing the onlookers to turn away in disgust.

He did like working alone, but going through a trash can behind an abandoned house first thing in the morning made him miss the companionship (and protection) of a partner. His thoughts were interrupted when he made a discovery near the bottom of the can.

After years of dumpster-diving, Cade had acquired the ability to zone out and search through regular trash without much thought. He could also spot important evidence from several feet away. It was similar to the way Veida listened to his stories.

Through the coffee filters and fast food wrappers, he spotted the camera Mr. Snow had offered in exchange for home protection. He scanned the area around him like a kid who found a dollar bill on the ground, looking to see if it was okay to snatch up the find.

Cade brushed away spaghetti, coffee grounds and a few remaining maggots. He realized the camera was useless on its own. There must be photos, or Larry wouldn't have known about the out-of-state tag. Or maybe he had told Snow about the Pennsylvania tag. He couldn't remember at the moment.

He returned to the stench of the garbage can and could now see the movement of the fly larva at the bottom. He knocked over the can and grabbed it underneath, dumping the remaining contents. Attached to the side of a spaghetti can, covered in sauce, was a narrow envelope. It was the kind a bank teller uses to give out cash. Cade knew it was his catch.

Back in the front seat of his Suburban, he didn't even take the time to wash off with the antibacterial he carried everywhere. He opened the envelope slowly, adding to the suspense, the same way he opened his high school report cards.

Several grainy photos were lodged inside, pasty with the residue of spaghetti sauce. They were the kind of pictures the little train at Chuck E. Cheese takes of children. They were printed on flimsy paper which added to the poor quality. Cade studied the top picture for a few moments to see the angle of the camera and the background in the photo. He looked back at the house to visualize the vantage point of the camera.

Cade removed the first few photos quickly and licked his fingers for better friction between photos six and seven. He paused in his treasure search only long enough to spit out his window. He chuckled at his own stupidity for ingesting what may have been a billion bacteria. Finally, there it was. The very last photo was an out-of-focus photo of his big, dark, mysterious car.

CHAPTER 15

Cade stood in front of Veida's desk in less than an hour. Although he was expected to maintain a telephone relationship with his lifeline, he needed the face-to-face interaction.

"Hold it yourself. I ain't catching no freakin' cooties for you or anybody else." He grabbed the envelope and showed the blurry photos to Veida, who immediately commented on the quality. As a joker and rarely serious guy, Cade sometimes had problems when he was ready to get serious and those he normally joked with weren't on his schedule.

"What do we have or who do we know that can enhance this?" Veida made a few telephone calls while Cade killed a million germs hanging on from Snow's.

"Have you even tried a magnifying glass, Sherlock?" Veida yelled out down the hall. "Check that top shelf in the file room. I think we have one of those little plastic, cube magnifying things you use to slide over photographs."

"Oh, yeah, photographs. What am I thinking?" Cade said, as he returned to Veida's desk without searching for the little plastic device. He snatched the pictures off Veida's desk without concern that he was re-infecting his hands with countless germs.

He made it to the interstate and pushed one hundred miles per hour as he glanced back and forth between phone and road. He hit send with the name *Gangloff* highlighted.

"Please tell me you're buying Moe's for lunch," Gangloff answered without concern for phone etiquette.

"Not a hello?"

"No, 'cause you only call when you need something."

"Actually, I was just calling to tell you I miss you and wonder if I could bring you lunch."

"Sure. I'm sitting right here waiting on the phone to ring." Cade hung up without a goodbye and pressed the accelerator a little closer to the floor. He took a minute to consider Gangloff's words and tried to think back to a time when he called with a lunch invite or just to say hello without asking for a favor. He then thought about calls to Lester and Veida and the other small number of people he called friends. Maybe he was a high-maintenance, self-absorbed friend.

He reached the parking lot of Gangloff's private investigation company in record time. He noticed the two cars parked in the lot and wondered if a client meeting would make conversation tough. He also took the time to consider that Gangloff's business must be doing well, because either car would be a better and more expensive vehicle than his own.

Gangloff and Cade had worked in the same office of a small federal agency during Cade's early years as an investigator. Gangloff was a little senior to Cade, so he paved the way as far as learning how to maneuver the federal system. Cade thought back to the time when he and Kelly spent nearly every weekend with Gangloff, who was always available to help the newly married couple with projects around the house. Gangloff had been so handy with a glue gun and shears, Cade thought he might have been gay. Turns out, he just enjoyed watching home makeover shows.

The government had sent Gangloff to several surveillance schools and even paid for advanced photography training. After becoming disenchanted with the government, Gangloff risked the steady government retirement to become a private investigator. He also opened a photography studio on the side for the more mundane photos like soccer teams and weddings. Cade respected the man for taking a risk he knew he couldn't.

Tim Gangloff was not only good, he was a perfectionist. He was happy and light-hearted and, typically, just fun to be around. He was one of the people on Cade's mind when he wrote the tactic involving effective people. The same one that Esposito had torn to pieces in Catfish's driveway.

With eyes squinting over the magnifying eyepiece,

Gangloff sat perfectly still. He moved only his right thumb and forefinger, focusing in on the picture.

"Has the government gone downhill since I left, Maddy? You'd think my tax dollars would buy better cameras. Think I could donate a new one and claim it on my taxes?"

Cade did not respond because he wanted Gangloff to focus without distraction. He hunched over a drafting board holding the same little plastic device Veida had suggested using. He switched from right eye to left and back again. Cade looked at one of Gangloff's many framed training certificates on the wall and tried to focus with his right eye, then left, conducting his own experiment to figure out why Gangloff kept changing eyes.

"It's definitely a Cadillac. Seville, I'd say. It does have a bar across the top and a lighter bar across the bottom. If this was a regular photo, I could blow it up a bit and even enhance it. This is probably a low res camera, like a VGA, and about a third a megapixel. Basically, this is probably more outdated than any government-issued camera out there."

"Good so far," Cade said, as a way to suggest he not give up.

"I can make out the letter S and C, and there might be a couple of ones in the number, but the brake lights are putting a shadow on both edges." Gangloff pulled the photo from under the magnifying glass as he asked about his payment for the effort. Cade dropped a handful of sunflower seeds on his desk.

"I guess this is lunch?" Gangloff asked, not surprised that Cade wouldn't stick around much longer than needed for the assistance.

"Why don't you call and invite me some time?" Cade said, as he turned for the door.

"You're welcome!"

"Thanks, man," Cade replied, as he stepped outside with a fresh lead to chase.

Cade dialed Veida before making it back to his car. He thought he knew how to manipulate Veida, but in typical female style, she let him think he was smart and had great negotiating skills.

"I have a challenge for you." Veida knew this sounded like work.

"Uh huh, I'm ready. You finally gonna let me give you that personality make over?"

"No," Cade fired back. "You finally gonna try that open mic night to share your comedy with the world?" Cade paused and was prepared to let Veida have the last word. She sensed the rushed tone of Cade's voice and let him continue. "I got a partial tag. I'm thinking, in all your free time, you can look for all Pennsylvania tags starting with SC and a couple of 1's in series."

"That's it?" Veida asked, challenging Cade in his level of optimism.

"You're the man," Cade shouted, as he disconnected the line. With not much to chase in the investigation, Cade decided a fishing trip was in order. Sure, he could sit in his office or in any number of police departments searching for Pennsylvania tags on Cadillacs, but Veida was one of the few people he would allow to chase a task without doing it over again or looking over her shoulder.

Although Cade didn't consider himself the smartest investigator, he always thought he could find the last piece of the puzzle when no one else could. The near hopeless search for the Cadillac would also give Cade a chance to get outside and clear his head. He had no idea if he was in the right ballpark, or even the right state. For nearly two solid hours, he drove Bankhead Highway, from Princeton Hospital to Adamsville, looking for a big Cadillac with Pennsylvania plates.

Because he possessed quite possibly the worst sense of direction in the world, Cade was only batting fifty percent on finding all six crime scenes. He knew if he called Veida for help, she'd assume he was fishing for a license plate update. He eventually gave up on finding the alley where Boxcar Shorty, aka, Doctor LNU victim number three was found. He called Veida hoping for a pick-me-up.

He really tried not to constantly bother Veida, but he could wait no longer. He came up with a good reason to call and hoped she'd offer some information.

"I just wanted to let you know I signed those closeout forms and sent them to the boss. You may want to intercept them to see if I did it right."

"Maddy, how long have you been sending in closed

case forms filled out wrong?" Cade knew he'd been busted.

"About three years, give or take," he replied.

"Yes, I do have some information on your school bus." Even under such serious circumstances, Veida wouldn't give up an opportunity to screw with Cade.

"School bus?" he shouted into the phone.

"Yeah, SC, that's Pennsylvania's two letter code for a school bus tag. I sure wish the witness would have just told you that in the beginning." Cade didn't remember the next twenty seconds of the call and later hoped he'd said goodbye this time.

Defeated and deflated, Cade decided on an unannounced stop by Uncle Frank's. He figured the visit would at least make him think of all the positive things in his life, since Esposito would probably be looking for a free lunch. It was no surprise that Uncle Frank hadn't a clue where his nephew might be.

He sat in the driveway thinking about some killer driving up in a Cadillac and making a miraculous confession. Because he didn't take boredom very well, he called Lester. He needed to tell Lester that the search for the Pennsylvania tag was a bust, but just as importantly, he needed to hear a friend's voice. Cade hoped Lester would increase his efforts to find the mysterious dark Cadillac. Lester was obviously in the middle of a call because he was a bit short with Cade. He failed to deliver even one insult.

Cade had only been sitting for about thirty minutes

when he saw a car headed directly his way. It wasn't a Cadillac, but it was a surprising sight. It was a little Mazda with a man in the passenger's seat holding copper pipes. The long pipes were lodged in his floorboard and sticking out the rear window. Cade was frustrated that he was wasting brain energy worrying how to keep Esposito out of trouble. The driver stayed not a second longer than necessary to get Esposito and his new found wealth out of his car.

"I didn't steal it, Maddy. They're tearing down that house on Roberta Road, and the owner said I could take anything I wanted." Cade decided to just ignore the entire theft of property discussion. The thought of Esposito still being involved in criminal activity and lying to one of the few people in the world trying to help him, frustrated Cade beyond repair, at least for the moment.

"I just dropped by to see that you're staying out of trouble, and I think you've answered that already. I need to get going." Esposito threw the copper on the side of Uncle Frank's house.

"I don't guess you can drive me and this scrap to ACIPCO can you? I'll buy you lunch for a change."

"I'm not putting stolen copper in my government vehicle, Ang. If you want me to drive you to pick up some job applications, I can do that. But if you're interested in living like a drug using thief, I'm not sure I can help you."

Esposito turned away from his old friend and

grabbed the handle of the rickety door. Cade knew tough love may not have been the right approach.

"Alright, Ang," he said, causing Esposito to stop just before entering the house. "I'll give you the benefit of the doubt on the copper, man. I'm just a little bummed because I thought I had a lead on a car in the case."

Esposito transformed from thief to part-time detective as he stepped off the porch headed to Cade's open window.

"What car? Where?"

"A couple witnesses have seen a Hispanic or light-skinned black man in a dark Cadillac at two of the crime scenes. It may be nothing. I don't know any more. But both witnesses said he had out-of-state license plates. One said it was Pennsylvania, which has a blue bar across the top and a yellow bar across the bottom. It's pretty freakin' distinct. Either the car had a colorful license plate protector on it, or the witness was smoking pot." Esposito walked closer to Cade with true interest.

"You can't find the plate in NCIC." Cade ignored the use of another term used only by the police.

"I only had the letters S and C, but my girl who runs the numbers says that's a school bus, so the witnesses were wrong. I've got somebody running all tags known to man, but it'll take some time." Esposito drummed his fingers on the hood of the dirty SUV. Even in Cade's frustrated state, he thought about the fact that Esposito didn't notice or care that he was getting his hands dirty.

"Listen, you need to get that stuff out of here, man, before they haul off Uncle Frank. I'll see you in a day or so." Cade left without looking back, but heard the clanking of the presumed stolen copper being moved out of sight. He cruised through the city's West Side for two more hours without a purpose or plan.

CHAPTER 16

Cade's cell phone vibrated in the center console for at least three rings before the sound registered in his swirling mind. The only people who lived in the 674 telephone prefix were his aunts, Cyndi and Ginger. Neither would call his cell phone unless someone died.

"Hey," Cade answered, expecting the worst.

"Is this Agent Cade?" the unknown voice asked.

"This is Maddy Cade. Who is this?" The unfriendly tone wasn't Cade's norm, but the day had been a bad one.

"This is Graysville's Mayor, Doug Brewer." Brewer was older than Cade, but the two considered themselves friends. Cade spent much of his childhood in Graysville at his grandmother's home, and the loose reigns of Grandma Mit allowed Cade to roam the city in search of all sorts of trouble. Brewer had grown up in Graysville and had never left. He was a celebrity of sorts, at least for small town standards. He was known by every citizen in the city and had served as the Christmas Parade Grand

Marshal for over five years running.

"Hey, Doug, sorry man, it's been a crappy day. What's the mayor of the year need from me?" Even though he sometimes thought it was funny how presidential Brewer acted, Cade would admit it was a pretty important feeling to call a mayor of any town by his first name.

"Maddy, listen," Brewer started, as Cade drifted off to imagine Brewer back in his days before City Hall. Brewer first made it big when he landed his own radio show. Cade wondered if the *mayor voice* was a throwback to his radio days or if it was really his own. He tried to think back to his teens and hear Brewer's voice in his mental storage of sounds.

After such a roller coaster day, Cade wasn't listening well to Brewer until he heard Esposito's name. He interrupted for a replay.

"Sorry, Doug, I lost you there for a minute. Start over."

"I was over at the P-D today and heard them talking about some warrants. Esposito's name came up. One of my guys said he heard Esposito was working with a fed he went to West Birmingham with. I figured that had to be you." Cade was beyond livid. Esposito wasn't even officially an informant, but somehow the mayor of a city not even involved in the Doctor LNU case knew of the connection.

"What's the warrant for?"

"I'll take that to mean yes, but its top secret," Brewer

said, still using his *on air* voice. "Why don't you give Chief Roberts a call tomorrow? We've got some hoodlums over by the old pharmacy, and I think Mr. Esposito may be able to help if you can convince him to sober up for fifteen minutes."

Cade asked for the chief's number because he had immediately decided he'd avoid becoming personally involved, and would simply pass along Esposito's number via a late-night voicemail message. He wanted to avoid personally speaking with the chief. He didn't want to end up with another Helena scenario.

Cade turned into his neighborhood in time to send Kelly out for another girls' night out. He slowed his pace to dial and leave a message for Chief Roberts and was surprised when a woman answered.

"I'm looking for Chief Roberts," Cade said, as he realized the mayor had freely given away the chief's home number.

"Hold on a second, hun," the woman said. Cade pictured the two having fried chicken and sweet potato pie for dinner.

"Hello," the gruff voice called out.

"Hey, Chief, sorry to get you at home. I thought I was calling your office."

"Now what in the Sam Hill would I be doing in the office at six o'clock?" Roberts barked out. Cade tried to decipher if his tone was serious.

"I heard you may have some issues with Angelo Esposito."

"Yep, you know where he's at?" Cade decided he didn't like the chief's tone, but figured he was just trying to impress his wife with the harshness.

"Yeah, he's where he's been for the past twenty years," Cade responded, taking the conversation to a near-confrontation level. He figured he could afford to tick off the chief since he could always count on his friend, the guy who signed the chief's paychecks, to smooth things over if he went too far.

By the end of the conversation, the two worked out their differences. Cade handed over the Esposito's home number just as easily as Mayor Brewer handed out the chief's. He figured he'd let Esposito handle this one on his own. He still had to decide if he wanted to stay mad at a guy who just may be too far gone for Cade to vouch for again.

Cade hit the door to the kitchen just in time to see Kelly glance up at the clock on the display of the double oven. She would be late for a second consecutive girly get-together.

Within fifteen minutes, she was out the door, and the kids were whining about the rubbery chicken nuggets Cade allowed to overcook in the microwave. In a rare show of frustration, Cade threw the chicken in the trash. He grabbed his keys and announced a trip to their local favorite, Area 41 Pizza. The kids were always up for Area 41, and Cade knew he'd have a chance to interact with someone other than a cop or recovering drug user.

After two plates of half eaten chicken fingers had

been removed from the table, the kids abandoned Cade for the call of the pizza joint's game room. Cade forced his favorite waiter to join him for his third UFO draft and meaningless conversation about anything other than an unsolved murder case.

Cade didn't know the waiter's last name. He felt certain the waiter didn't know his either since he usually called him *dog*. Cade thought of Randy Jackson from that panel of judges every time Allan greeted him with, "What's up, dog?" and a knuckle punch. This was a great escape for Cade.

His cell phone buzzed during a deep discussion of last weekend's "crunked up par-tay" at Allan's house. He hit the *do not answer* key and returned to the waiter's tale. Before finishing his story, Allan was called away to another table. Cade waved and mouthed, *see you later*. Allan pressed his fist over his heart and then flashed that stupid sideways peace sign. He actually looked cool doing it.

Cade rounded up the kids and made it home past everyone's bed time. The house phone rang just as he was pulling back the covers. He grabbed it before the second ring so as not to wake his son.

"What?" is all he offered, knowing it was Esposito. He wanted to ensure that Esposito knew he was still mad because of his refusal to avoid trouble. Cade remembered the call to the chief and figured Esposito was looking for some advice.

"Maddy, I owe you one, man. Chief Roberts called,

and I'm going down there tomorrow. Mom's gonna take me. He said they can take care of my tickets and even pay me a little if I'll work some deals for them." Cade let it all sink in. He felt a little concerned for the first time that he was putting his neck on the line too much for Esposito.

"They're going to take me to the Alabama Motel, and I'm gonna call them knuckleheads who used to sell weed down there by the tennis courts. You remember Tim Bridgemont and those clowns?" Cade refused to share in the excitement.

"Why are you calling on the house phone?" Cade asked in a tone meant to show his frustration.

"I called your cell, and you didn't answer," Esposito answered in his continuing upbeat voice.

In the same frustrated tone, Cade said, "I didn't answer because I couldn't talk. That's why voicemail was invented."

Esposito must have known Cade needed time to get over his frustration because he jumped right to the point of the call with only a slight attempt at humor.

"So, Maddy, are you too mad for me to tell you about your Birmingham Southern tag?"

"What?" Cade thought it was odd for Esposito to be sharper than him so late at night, but wrote it off to the beer.

"Your Cadillac."

It hit Cade hard. Birmingham Southern College. The missing letter was B. No one had questioned the witness who was sure he'd seen a Pennsylvania tag. The blue and yellow stripes were almost identical to the college's personalized tag. Why in the world had that not been obvious to Cade or Lester or any other cop worth anything at all?

"How'd you know that?" Cade couldn't help but ask.

"Do you know how much dope I've bought around Southern? The P-D won't let the narcs spend the extra money for personalized tags, so the college tags are always a safe bet." Cade quickly dismissed Esposito's use of the present tense, *are always*. He was rubbing his temples and wanting to high five someone.

"Good luck with Graysville. I'll call you later."

CHAPTER 17

Cade intended to wake before dawn, but the mixture of draft beer and Birmingham Southern news made going to sleep nearly impossible. Once asleep, waking on time was even harder. Cade showered in record time and made back-to-back phone calls to Veida and Lester to request the tag search. He left the bedroom in search of clothes that he assumed would be stacked in the laundry room. He felt a bit of guilt that he hadn't done a load of laundry in months. He swore to himself he'd return to a normal level of family participation when the doctor was behind bars.

He was surprised to see Kelly in the kitchen, rushing around as if headed to a big meeting. She yelled for Madelyn, who was most likely in her room experimenting with makeup. He couldn't remember when she'd started using it, but he hadn't been in on the approval process and kept forgetting to talk with Kelly about it.

"You're dripping on my clean floor," she said as she

motioned for him to stand close. He instinctively tried to flex his chest to take full advantage of being half naked. There were a lot of things he missed by staying out so late chasing killers. "I'll make you a deal," she said with a look that told her husband he wanted the deal. "You make it home during school hours and I'll make it worth your while." She pulled him into her and kissed him passionately to reinforce the offer.

The familiar buzz from the kitchen table meant Veida was returning his call.

"This could be big," he said, as he turned his back to her. He flipped open the phone, stopping its vibration. Kelly didn't seem to care who was calling or if they could hear her.

"Is it as big as the meeting I have with Madelyn's principal today? She just got tapped into the National Honor Society. I didn't even waste my breath inviting you to the ceremony. I also didn't invite you to Donavan's doctor's appointment this afternoon. Your son has an ear infection." Cade just stood with his hand over the phone's mouthpiece as Madelyn made it downstairs and out the door without a word to her father. He noticed she had an excess of mascara on but he knew he was in no position to comment. Donavan, who had been sitting nearby on the couch during the near makeout session, slowly stood and followed his mother with one hand over his ear.

"Bye, Dad, the smaller version of Cade whispered." Cade just waved to his son. He returned to Veida.

"You owe me big," Veida said in her most bragging tone. "5400 Bankhead Highway in Birmingham." Cade wrote the info on the palm of his hand.

"What's the name?" He asked, as he pulled on his jeans.

"Um, Daily Automotive." Cade's elation gave way to a possible obstacle. If the car was a lease or loaner, it could be another exciting lead that ended in frustration.

Cade made a second call to Lester while driving down the emergency lane of Hwy 280, past the wreck at the entrance to Starbucks. He knew the car dealership wouldn't go anywhere, and it didn't matter if he arrived within the next few minutes or few days, but he could not resist speeding toward the possible conclusion to the case.

Lester's immediate voicemail pickup indicated he was on the phone. He was probably trying to get the same information already recovered by Veida. Cade left an unusually short message.

"Daily Automotive. It's by Milo's, I think. I know it's out of your beat, so take the wife's station wagon if you need to, but meet me there."

Cade pulled into Daily's just after nine, and his was the only car on the lot. The bright yellow trailer that once served as the dealership office appeared empty, if not abandoned, but if so, the retreating owners had left furniture and files behind. Cade searched the windows, doors and anything he could see through the windows for any clues to a contact number or even first name of Mr. or Mrs. Daily.

In the reflection from a broken clock hanging on the paneled wall, Cade could see the red blinking light of a motion detector mounted above the door. He grabbed the door knob and positioned his foot for a kick that would be sure to set off the alarm. He was interrupted by a Jefferson County Sheriff's patrol car speeding from across the highway at the sight of a possible vandal. As the county cruiser scraped the steep embankment of the parking lot driveway, Cade slowly grabbed his badge from his rear pocket. The deputy seemed to look disappointed that there would be little action.

"Hey, man," Cade said, as he searched his memory for names matching the name tag, Brumaker.

"What you doing?" the deputy questioned, as he took a defensive stance. He didn't seem to notice or care about the badge in Cade's hand.

"I have a lead on a case that ends here. I need to find the folks who own this place," Cade said, with his best sense of urgency, but not emergency. Behind Brumaker, Cade saw Lester driving by at a slow speed. The look on his face said, *I got your message, but I'm way out of my area.* He knew Lester wasn't going to mess with Jefferson County.

"Joe Daily died a few years ago. Had a heart attack right here in this parking lot. It was the craziest thing. I was..." Cade knew he'd seem terribly insensitive but simply could not stand to wait for the details of Mr. Daily's demise.

"Hey, man, I'm sorry, but I'm real anxious about

this one. Do you know who runs this place? I really need to take a look at some files." Deputy Brumaker seemed only slightly insulted.

"His stupid boy took over. Ain't got the sense God gave a duck." Cade saw the image of his grandmother telling him Tim Bridgemont didn't have the sense God gave a goose, and he wondered who had the old saying right. He figured Mit was right for sure.

Cade focused again on Brumaker and realized he didn't miss anything important.

"He don't sell many cars, but he hangs out over at the other lot on Finley Avenue. I think he might be using the place to sell dope."

"Great, man. Thanks a lot!" Cade had no idea where the lot was, but he felt the need to avoid bringing too many chefs into the kitchen. He headed toward Finley Avenue while looking for Lester on his cell phone's call log. Only one ring this time.

"Man, what are you stirring up now?" Lester asked without a hello.

"I'm headed to some car lot owned by a Joe Daily. It's on Finley. Do you know the place?" Lester was slow to answer. He seemed to pause because he wanted to ask what was going on and not because he was trying to place the dealership.

"It's across from Costa's, but closer to the Farmer's Market."

"I'll see you there," Cade said, without asking if Lester could make it. Cade pulled into yet another vacant car lot where another old trailer sat. This one was bright red. Lester pulled in directly behind Cade. He stopped inches behind Cade's SUV and raised his hands as if complaining that Cade was running him all over town. Cade, sensing that they may be waiting for a while for Daily, grabbed a bag of jalapeño sunflower seeds from the passenger seat. He got out and faced Lester.

"The Cadillac. It was sold by this guy," Cade said, pointing at a sign that once read "Daily's Deals." The sign had been modified to read "Daily sux," thanks to a talented graffiti artist. "But from his other lot in Forestdale. Do you know this guy, Daily?" Cade again took the time to realize he was rushing for no good reason. There was no evidence about to be lost or lives wasted if he didn't find Mr. Daily immediately.

Lester offered no suggestions, so Cade turned his attention to the doors and windows of the small trailer. A business card was lodged inside the window closest to the door. It was the card of a security consulting company. Cade grabbed the card and flipped open his cell phone.

"I-A-T," the base voice announced.

"Hi, this is Special Agent Maddison Cade." It was a seldom used title and name combo. "I need some help finding Joe Daily of Daily Automotive on Finley Avenue. I think you may have installed his security system."

"Well, old man Daily's been dead for nearly a year. You're probably looking for his son, Jimmy." Cade was interrupted by the sound of a car in need of a water pump. It circled the trailer headed in his direction.

"I think I'm good, man. Thanks a lot." Cade hung up without hearing a goodbye.

"What's going on?" the young man asked.

"You Jimmy?" Cade asked, trying not to sound too threatening.

"Yep, the county said somebody was looking for my dad," Daily said, as he looked through a set of keys that would make a high school janitor proud. Daily opened the door, and the three men filled the tiny space within. Cade wondered if three were the most people who had ever been inside the Daily Sales Center at one time.

Daily opened the bottom drawer of his desk. He pulled a large revolver from the back of his pants to store inside. Both law enforcers in the room watched with little concern. Daily moved slowly to display the weapon as if the law enforcers would feel they all had something in common.

"So what's up, gentlemen?" Daily asked, as he leaned back in a chair that surely was older than him. Lester didn't even make eye contact. He wanted Cade to know he was expected to do the talking.

"We're looking for the owner of a dark blue 1999 Cadillac registered here." Daily didn't give it more than a few seconds of thought.

"Don't know. How is it that you think it was one of my cars?" As Cade opened his mouth to answer, he knew he'd been stupid to think the car may have been sold with a Birmingham Southern tag. He felt a little silly but marched on.

"The car belongs to a possible witness, not a subject," Cade said, in case Daily knew the owner and was just trying to protect him. "The tag on the car is a Birmingham Southern tag registered to your dad's Forestdale lot." Daily unfolded his arms, which was a good sign to both cops. He leaned forward on the old wooden desk and part-time gun locker.

"So I'd say the DMV screwed up and let some dillweed use the sales receipt or some of our other paperwork as their address. We ain't never registered no tag, period."

Daily stood and turned away from both men. "If dad sold it from Forestdale, I've got the paperwork. He only sold a dozen or so cars out of that crap stand. All the receipts are in a little shoe box in here."

Daily entered the even smaller back room of the trailer. Both Cade and Lester moved to keep an eye on Daily as they were trained to do, but neither considered the young salesman a threat. From the back room, Daily started talking in between the grunts and strains as he shifted and sorted through an array of unorganized boxes.

"Problem is, guys, based on my typical clientele, I have a stated policy of not releasing nothing to the law without a court order."

Cade was surprised by the words because they were in total contradiction to Daily's actions and demeanor. He emerged from the poorly lit room with a small shoe box labeled *Sales*, handwritten in red marker. He dropped the small box on his desk.

"I can't give you guys this, cause that'd mean I was jerkin' around with my customers, and we got something here called the Daily Word." Both Cade and Lester stood in dismay at the man's comments. Lester grabbed Cade by the arm and tugged in the direction of the door, but it was clear to Cade that Daily wasn't finished. "Looky here, I gotta go 'round to the bathroom. I can't let you guys in this little box. I'm sure you understand." Daily opened the front door and both Cade and Lester realized there was no working bathroom inside the old trailer. Daily was going to relieve himself behind the office. "Nice meeting you two. I may be a while," Daily said. He closed the door without waiting for a reply.

"You need to go get a Subpoena, man," Lester said like a law school professor. "If you take anything outta there now, it's gonna get tossed in court." He adjusted his work belt and headed to the door behind Daily. Cade couldn't remember Lester ever doing anything prudent like thinking ahead to possible court testimony. Lester stopped short of the front steps and turned toward Cade, still holding the doorknob. "You nearly got me busted the last time you pulled me off my beat. I ain't gonna step in it for any goon like you," he said, with just the right touch of sarcasm. Cade hesitated for a second or two before opening the shoe box. Lester turned to leave, then back again as if he forgot something. Cade looked from his stack of papers only briefly to acknowledge Lester.

"What's up with Angelo? Are you still letting him hang around? I don't trust him, man, and people are starting to think he's using you."

"What people," Cade asked, sounding a bit too defensive.

"I'm not telling you how to handle your informants, just be careful. I see him nearly every day, riding that stupid bicycle and hustling up money for a fix. You're not out here in the trenches, federal man. He's trouble. I promise you that."

Cade was torn between defending Esposito and venting to Lester about how he had been getting the run-around from Esposito. He figured he really didn't have the time for either, so he just nodded to show Lester he heard him out.

Lester left Cade to his work and pulled out of the parking lot, accelerating quickly, as if he'd gotten a call or inquiry about his *out of service*. Lester's words replayed in his mind, and the thought kept him from his work. *He's trouble. I promise you that.* He shook it off and returned to Daily's shoe box.

CHAPTER 18

"Bingo! There you are, Mr. Chan Ming, owner of one gently loved 1999 Cadillac DeVille. Could you be my guy?" Cade started to memorize the social security number and date of birth, but grabbed a nearby pen for assurances. He wrote the first three numbers of Ming's social security number on his hand then thought how embarrassing it would be to have to return after a sweaty ride to Ming's house washed away his lead. He'd have to ask Daily to go pee in the backyard again.

He wrote every number and identifying mark from the paper onto a bright pink sticky note he pulled from Daily's top drawer. He put the box back in order and left it for Daily to put back in its proper place. As he pulled from the driveway seconds later, Cade could see Daily leaning against the side of the trailer smoking a cigarette while he waited for the cops to move on.

He picked up the cell phone to call Officer Preston, his only contact in the West Precinct. He needed any intelligence available on Ming or his home which was located by the Forestdale Methodist Church about ten miles away. After the first ring, Cade thought better of telling anyone about the strongest hope of finding a suspect since the beginning of the case. He disconnected the line and dialed Lester instead.

"Go," Lester answered, as if a soldier in the heat of battle.

"I got it. Can you hook up with me?" Cade asked, but it was only a formality as he knew Lester would have his back.

"Dude, you're killing me. You trying to get me fired? I'm not a detective anymore and can't be stepping all over the other precincts. You got a name and address? I'll see if anybody knows the mope, but I can't go."

Cade opened the palm of his hand before realizing he'd deviated from his norm and had actually written the details on paper.

"Mr. Chan Ming. 1212 Cedar Crest Drive. And by the way, this latest development makes me hungry for Chinese buffet. I wanna keep the Mingster just between us for now until we can scope out the place. I don't need too many bystanders on this one, you know." Lester cleared his throat.

"Mad, I can't sneak that far out this time of the day. The lieutenant will skin me. He's already made some snide comments about me holding your hand on this thing. I really don't need to get crossed up with him."

Cade ignored the insult and focused on his

speedometer as it hit ninety. He barely had time to concoct a plan before making it to Cedar Crest Drive. The house could clearly be seen from Cedar Crest, but due to the large front windows of the home, Cade was reluctant to turn into the long, unprotected driveway. He pulled onto the road's shoulder to get a better look before driving straight to his suspect without even a plan of action. In a last minute rational thought, Cade veered back onto Cedar Crest to regroup and formulate a real plan.

It took twenty minutes of wasted day to reach the checkout at the Kangaroo Mart, and that included the five it took to pick out a dozen doughnuts. It was just past eleven o'clock when he made it to Uncle Frank's. He thought he might have to wake up Esposito but was surprised to see him sitting on the front porch with Skip halfway on his lap.

When Cade got out of the car, the only reaction to his presence was the slow wag of Skip's tail. Skip was certainly more excited than his owner to see Cade. He walked past Esposito and his dog and took the doughnuts inside to Uncle Frank who was cursing at how the poorly the Atlanta Braves were playing in a game that took place sometime during the eighties. Cade slipped a couple of doughnuts from the box and gave the rest to Uncle Frank. The man paused his baseball critique long enough to thank Cade.

Cade quietly returned to Esposito and handed him the doughnuts. Esposito took them without a word. He knew it was a token of peace only until the next screw up or questioned act. He tore off a piece and gave it to Skip, and both ate like they hadn't eaten in a while. The dog's head rested on Esposito's lap. A dirty rope hung around the dog's neck. Cade instinctively loosened the make-shift collar. Esposito was again the one to break the silence.

"That's what I need, Maddy, somebody to loosen the noose. I can't breathe, and I can't see myself living a normal life, going to a job, that kind of thing. Maybe it's too late for me, man."

After a deep sigh, Cade spoke. His eyes stayed focused on the cigarette butts in the gravel at his feet.

"I need your help with the doctored drugs, and I don't have time to decide if you've been lying to me. I don't know if you're clean or if you even want to be." Esposito took the opening line better than anticipated.

"I've told you before I'm doing the best I can, and I'll do anything for you, man." Cade stood, figuring Esposito would continue his talk about recovery during the trip to Cedar Crest.

"Bring the pooch too, I guess," Cade said, as he looked through the screen door. Uncle Frank had fallen asleep. "Will your uncle be okay?"

"Of course," Esposito said, as he scooped Skip up in his arms. "See you in a bit, Frankie," he yelled at the house.

The drive back to Cedar Crest took less than twenty minutes. It took him even less time to deliver the poorly thought out plan to Esposito. It wasn't as much poorly thought out as it was *not* thought out.

"I can only drive up that driveway one time without raising suspicion. If it still looks like nobody's home, I'm going to drop you in the back behind their garage. I want you to just wait for something to happen that can get me in that house. I need to be able to say to a judge that it's probable there is some piece of evidence in there. *Probable* is the key. Not a guess or hunch, but something I can use in a little show-and-tell with the judge."

Cade approached the driveway quickly, giving Esposito little time to ask questions.

"What if..." Cade interrupted Esposito in an effort to avoid hearing any plan that may violate the law. He looked directly into Esposito's eyes and spoke slowly and deliberately.

"You will stay in the car and out of sight until I'm done at the door. If nobody wants to chat, I'll drop you off on the way out and you will hide out back until the cows come home or until something moves. You will find me probable cause to get into that house, and you won't do anything illegal."

Cade knocked on the door and on at least eight windows for no less than five minutes. He could see through a couple of windows, but nothing of value was spotted. He returned to his vehicle and the anxious Esposito. He reached behind his seat, inside a duffle bag filled with several gadgets and surveillance necessities, and retrieved a cell phone. It was the pay-as-you-go, no frills version. "Turn it on and the volume off. I'll call you in a while. Do not even think about making any calls."

Cade didn't even stop fully as Esposito jumped to the grass with Skip in his arms.

"Let Skip go," Cade said in his loudest whisper, "and if you get caught, tell whoever finds you that you were just looking for him." Esposito seemed to love the plan and nodded in agreement as if the suggestion to bring Skip was a brilliant idea.

As Cade rounded Ming's, he saw movement at the neighbor's house. The small home was clearly visible through the vacant lot covered with a few scraggly pine trees. He decided a drive to the neighbor's, under the pretext of a solicitation, might be an opportunity to gather information. It would also make him appear to be a door-to-door salesman should someone in the Ming house be watching.

Cade worried that Esposito may be confused by his actions. He was used to making a plan as he went along, so didn't think twice about a spur of the moment visit to a second home without a specific purpose in mind. As he parked in front of Ming's neighbor's house, Cade caught a quick glimpse of Esposito sprawled out behind Ming's garage like an Army Ranger. Skip was hovering nearby as if he was waiting on information about the game his owner had started.

Simultaneous movement at the neighbor's house returned Cade's attention to the brick split-level. As he slid down from the driver's seat, he could clearly see now that the movement was that of a young boy. The child was playing in a sandbox under the side porch of the brick home. After closer examination, still from thirty feet away, Cade could see the boy had what was most likely Down Syndrome. He seemed mentally impaired too, based on his sounds and movements.

As he was being confronted by a large man, it occurred to Cade he should have known an adult wouldn't be too far from the boy.

"He's got a great little hideaway down there," Cade said as an icebreaker. The man held a rake and was apparently not in the mood for chit chat.

"What do you need?"

Unfortunately, Cade started this conversation like most of his conversations, without a game plan. This was the norm for Cade because he was confident in his ability to think on his feet. But seeing the young boy sidetracked Cade a bit. At the moment, he thought nothing would make him happier than to sit with the kid and play cars in the sand. After a long pause, he opened his mouth without thinking.

"I'm trying to meet folks in the area who may like to sit down and make sure all their insurance needs are being met," he said in his most passionate insurance salesman voice.

"We ain't interested. We got our hands full with all the paper and insurance forms now with our little man there." Both men looked at the boy, who was now making incoherent bursts of sound as he rammed his cars into each other.

"To-to-to-to," the boy shouted.

"He sure is full of energy," is all Cade could find to say as he thought about his escape. The man sighed and relaxed a bit, as if he was so tired he could lay in the freshly-raked leaves for a nap.

"He plays with those cars from sun up 'til sun down. The favorite one is the police car. We think he might have seen one on a cop show or something. He crashes that one into all the other cars."

"Yeah," was all Cade could muster as he nodded at the man.

"Before we bought this place, we lived by the police department in Tarrant. I drove a truck up 'til last week, so I wasn't home much. The wife says he used to stand by the window for hours just to see the police drive by. I guess they stuck in his head. I can't figure him out. He's in his own world."

Watching the little boy took Cade back to his summers working at Camp ASCCA near Auburn University. ASCCA is a camp for kids and adults with all sorts of disabilities. Many of Cade's campers were mentally disabled. He remembered those summers as being the best time of his life. Probably because it's hard to feel down when you're taking care of someone with no legs, or a kid with no control over his muscles, or one who doesn't even know he's part of the world.

"To-to-to-to." Cade came to and looked at the defender of the little boy. The man was now propped on his rake staring at the boy as if he were picturing him running around a baseball diamond or catching a pass.

"Nice talking with you, sir," Cade said. "Take care of the little man there." He returned to his car which looked nothing like an insurance agent's car.

"Take care now," the man said, as he slowly returned to his raking.

Turning back onto Cedar Crest Drive, he realized he'd failed to discuss the pickup arrangements with Esposito. He reached for his phone but was relieved, and a little surprised, to see Esposito, walking at a fast pace away from Ming's, nearly a hundred yards away. Esposito spotted Cade as he approached and quickly picked up his fuzzy partner and returned to the safety of his passenger seat.

"I got in," Esposito nearly yelled before Cade could stop him.

"I said don't do anything illegal which would include breaking and entering! What did you find?" Esposito seemed to be totally confused by Cade's mission statement, or lack thereof. He eventually caught on that Cade's response was a *covering his butt* comment.

"Nothing. Somebody was there. It reminded me of the time Yolanda's dad came home and I jumped out her bedroom window like a cat burglar." Cade let the stupidity of his decision sink in.

"Did they see you?"

"No," Esposito quickly responded with assurance. "No way. So what's next?" Esposito asked as if he was in for the duration.

"I'm dropping you and Skippy off, and I'm back here until I see something that means something." The time display on the radio meant afternoon traffic may soon pick up. Cade slowly increased his speed, hoping Ming didn't show up after being out and about. Esposito seemed to realize he was about to get pushed off the team and he scrambled for a comeback.

"Hey, I got a new bike yesterday. I forgot to tell you. Somebody stole the *Grey Goose* so I had to get another mode of transportation until I get my license back. It's a twelve-speed, so I can make it over here with no problem if you need me to."

Cade did not spend one second thinking about how Esposito lost his *Grey Goose,* what a Grey Goose was exactly, or how he acquired a new twelve-speed. He spent very little time wondering where Esposito may have found the money for a new bike or from which unsecured garage he may have *found* it.

Cade realized he was lucky to have gotten out of this mission unscathed. He decided he'd work it out the old fashioned way. He prepared himself for long, boring surveillance.

CHAPTER 19

After dropping Esposito back at the quasi-safety of his mother's house, Cade called Lester to brief him on the Ming house visit. He conveniently left out the part about Esposito breaking about three laws. A modified version of the break and enter violation was left on Lester's voicemail.

The call to Lester was immediately followed by a call to Kelly explaining he wouldn't be home any time soon. She seemed to take it in stride and said she and the kids would go to Jim 'N Nick's. Remembering that he hadn't eaten all day, Cade reached for a bag of sunflower seeds to keep his mind off his favorite barbeque.

Eight solid hours and not one movement from within the Ming home. No lights, no cars, nothing. He wanted to call it a night, but knew he'd feel guilty if he left. He figured he wouldn't be able to sleep anyway. Before he could finish the pro-versus-con list in his head, his phone vibrated in the center console.

Cade usually called Lester, not the other way around.

So Lester's number on the phone display at nearly 10 p.m. meant possible good news to Cade.

"Hey, man," Cade answered.

"You still sittin' on that house?"

"Yeah, you want to reconsider? It's a party over here." Cade hadn't felt like joking around in a while.

"So that means you're sitting down, right?" Lester spoke with purpose, as if he was building up to something huge.

"Bring it, man," Cade said. He was practically begging for good news.

"I found your Asian guy. He's toast, brother. Like extra crispy. House fire over on 16th and Lomb, by Princeton. It's not too far from Snow's place." Lester gave him a few seconds to let it sink in. Cade started the engine and slammed the gas pedal against the floorboard, headed in Lester's direction.

"Who I-D'd Ming?"

"Nobody, but I talked with one of the water boys who said they had two dead inside, one Asian and one black dude. He also said they had to back out and suit up in hazmat gear after the first guys in got sick. He said they found some strange lab in the kitchen, and I put two and two together. Plus, it helps that your Cadillac is in the carport." Cade didn't know if he should be celebrating or cursing. "One more thing," Lester continued, "a bike was in the carport too, and I think it's your boy's. He's tied up in this thing somehow, Maddy."

Cade kept one eye on the speedometer, now pushing eighty, as he headed west toward Princeton Hospital.

"Are you sure no one else is in the house?" Cade asked, wondering to himself if he was concerned about Esposito, or if he wanted the chance to kick his butt personally.

"I don't know, man. I'll try to find out and wait for you here."

Cade arrived in the middle of fire trucks, a couple of ambulances, and at least eight marked units. He snapped his badge on his jeans and started his search for the bicycle Lester tipped him off about.

There it was, leaning against the Cadillac with both tires melted and the seat still smoking. Even in its condition, Cade could see the men's Mongoose bicycle had once been grey. He'd been hoping it was not part of the fire. On the way over, he had concluded that the only possible explanation was that, somehow, Esposito heard of the fire and rode over out of curiosity. The fact that the bicycle recognized by Lester was the "stolen" bike, and not the new twelve-speed, gave him a touch of nausea.

A firefighter put his thickly gloved hand on Cade's chest.

"You can't go any further, man, the place is charcoal."

"Who's in charge?" Cade asked in a way that said he needed help, and not that he was about to try to boss someone around.

"Captain Majors. I'll send him over. And who are you?"

"I'm working the doctor case," Cade offered to the firefighter, figuring that was far more important than his name or title.

"Oh cool, man. You think we got Doctor Death in there?" Cade didn't know whether to answer the question or ask if the case was now being called Doctor Death by everyone except the case agent.

Cade showed more proper credentials to the captain and even gave him one of the business cards he distributed so sparingly. The captain promised to call with a full description of all properties and people inside including a full list of any drug and chemical containers or labels if found.

Lester was nowhere to be found. He must have received another call. Cade could only stand by with the growing crowd as the fire department kept full control of the scene. He couldn't handle the role of an onlooker, so he decided to go to the office and start some of his mandatory paperwork. No need to get home now, he thought. The family would be asleep, and his brain wouldn't allow that for at least a few hours anyway.

He was less than a mile from the fire scene before the nausea returned. It was brought on by the probability of Esposito's involvement in the case. Cade decided maybe his job security was more important than any bond the two once shared. He made a decision to distance himself from Esposito as much as possible and hope their joint efforts weren't noticed by anyone other than Lester.

Taking on the role of one of his suspects, Cade subconsciously began crafting explanations for Esposito's actions. He visualized himself standing in front of his supervisor's desk, explaining that he was just about to complete the paperwork necessary to make Esposito an informant. H e could carefully articulate that because Esposito wanted to make such a good impression, he got too close to the targets. He prayed no evidence was uncovered that put any different spin on the situation.

Cade drove nearly twenty miles in a daze before his vibrating cell phone woke him fully. An unknown number flashed on the display.

"Maddison Cade."

"Special Agent Cade?" Captain Majors asked. Cade cringed at hearing his formal title. "The bodies will be shipped over to Cooper Green. I'm sure you've been working with those guys, so they should jump right on it. We found some bottles still in one piece. They might be able to use 'em for comparison. There was a guy in the back room with no identification. He's pretty crisp, so it may take some time. There was a Chinese guy in the kitchen. His name is Chan Tsu Ming. Maybe he's your chef. His wallet is totally melted, but we recovered some stuff from the glove compartment of the Cadillac."

"Thanks. Send me what you can when you can. I'll hook up with Dr. Justice."

"Mention me at the press conference, okay?" The captain was another to point out the stereotype of federal agencies planning more press events than successful case operations. Cade didn't feel the need to respond.

Before Cade could hang up, he heard a beep signaling a second incoming call. Strange that his phone would ring back-to-back calls so late, especially if his agency hadn't had time to receive word of the deaths. The phone's display identified his home number. Cade clicked off the captain and clicked on the captain of his house.

"Hey, babe. You alright?" Cade asked, because she rarely called him during work.

"Yeah, I was going to ask you the same thing. Your case is all over the news." He couldn't recall seeing news crews at the fire and wondered how he'd escaped without questioning.

"Are the kids asleep?" Cade asked, realizing he had asked his wife that question far too many times. She was forced into single parent mode way too often because of his work habits.

"Yeah, and you-know-who is in your spot again."

"I'll see you in a bit," he said, knowing he wouldn't see her until morning.

With everyone in his house going to sleep, Cade knew he had even less reason to return home right away. He fought one last urge to turn around and seek out Esposito. He finally rationalized that nothing good could come from finding Esposito at the moment. The worst that could happen would involve fighting the desire to go ahead and kill his old friend and get it over with. He was, however, eager to hear Esposito's explanation of how his bicycle ended up at the bond fire.

Cade's head was pounding with thoughts of Ming, Esposito, Pooky, Big Pimpin and the others. He was reluctant to go to bed because the ton of pending paperwork would no doubt make it into his dreams. Mainly because he loathed paperwork in general, but also because he knew the case wasn't close to being over. Instead, it had just passed one major hurdle.

Even with the probable identification of the doctored drug maker, Cade knew everyone in his agency, and most of the city, would be looking for a final report or a final announcement that the mystery was solved. For Cade, finding Ming was only half the puzzle. The other half, the half that may never be known, was why.

It was nearly midnight when he turned the deadbolt on his warehouse office. He started with the more routine forms, most of which he could complete without much thought. Within an hour, he had completed all the forms for a Summary Report. He left a few required forms for later. They would require far more creativity than he could muster.

Now nearly ready to fight for space in his bed, Cade was startled by the vibrating of his cell phone. He felt bad that he misjudged Kelly's actions. She had obviously stayed awake to wait for him.

"Hey. Sorry. I thought you'd be asleep," Cade said in true regret.

"Who can sleep in here?" Esposito said like it was the middle of the day. Cade took the receiver away from his ear to look at the display which was gone. He returned to the earpiece. The familiar echo of men yelling in the background was déjà vu to Cade.

"Screw you, Angelo! I can't do it anymore! You're tearing me down, man."

"What?" Esposito offered in protest for such a strong statement. "It's a stupid trespassing thing, man. The guy at the Kangaroo hates me and had me picked up. I was just walking through his parking lot, minding my own business. Lester even said he hated to pick me up, but that idiot said he thought I was a danger to his customers." It was the final straw for Cade, and he launched the inquisition. He had little concern for Esposito at this point, but his own name and career were on the line. Further, Cade immediately pictured and dreaded the conversation with Lester who would certainly have some *I told you so* advice for him.

"Why were you walking and not on your new bike, Ang?" Cade asked with a clinched jaw as he replayed Esposito's conversation about buying the new bike.

"What do you mean? I was walking because my bike got stolen. What are you getting at, Mad? What's the big deal?" It didn't take the veteran agent a full second to piece together a broken timeline confirming that Esposito was lying. For some reason Cade would later question in his own mind, he hung up on Esposito. He decided to wash his hands of the whole thing. The thought that Lester had been the one to pick him up was salt in the wound.

Cade leaned back in his chair and rubbed his temples with both hands. He thought if he sat still long enough, he could make the whole thing go away. The cases, the paperwork, the lying drug addict, the whole mess would just disappear.

CHAPTER 20

A small pain in Cade's lower back slowly brought him back to reality. He opened his eyes to the paperwork still spread across his desk. He felt sick that he'd stayed in his office all night and wondered if Kelly and the kids were awake. He reached for his cell phone to check the time. At some point in the night, the phone had fallen to the floor. The front did not display the time but rather the announcement of four missed calls. His sick feeling worsened.

He deleted the first two messages after hearing only the first two words of an automated operator asking if he'd accept a collect call from the city jail. The next two were from his supervisor. The boss wanted to meet to discuss the agency's planning of a press event. He pictured Captain Majors' unhappy expression. He would call Kelly later to apologize. Maybe he'd start planning that getaway to the beach they needed so badly and miss the press conference entirely.

Cade changed into his standby slacks and shirt that

had been hanging behind his office door untouched for nearly six months. He begrudgingly headed to the less than desirable Pancake King on the other side of town. It was a meeting spot picked by his supervisor months prior for last-minute meeting needs just like this one. As he climbed back into his office on wheels, his tight slacks made him realize that the daily fast food lunches and decreasing metabolism were taking a toll on his waistline.

The thoughts of a few extra pounds, Esposito being back in jail, and his boss who was about to ask for a timeline on the case closure was too much to handle. He needed to get straight before seeing his boss. In his present condition, he was likely to snap at the wrong guy. He had taken the back road to connect to I-65 in an effort to arrive before the boss, but his brain wouldn't stop churning.

He pulled off the highway in front of Chelsea High School's impressive practice football field which was full of students enjoying some recess activity. The sight of teenagers without a care in the world was usually therapeutic for Cade. Today though, they just reminded him of his quickly approaching forty-second birthday.

They also made him question just how much he was really contributing to society. He envied the kids for their youth and for having so many opportunities ahead of them. He hoped when Madelyn made it to the school, she'd get him invited to some career day or government classes so he could tell them personally.

The familiar vibration of his cell phone ended Cade's self-deprecating trance. He listened as an assistant to the fire caption explained that city forensics trained detectives were going over the charred remains of the 16th Street house in the morning light. Already, a large quantity of an unknown substance was being hand delivered to Dr. Justice for comparison. The fact that the local police had done very little on this case until after a killer was found would have normally infuriated Cade, but this time, for some reason, he didn't care if they announced the analysis at their own press conference and convinced the world they'd been working on the case sixteen hours a day.

Cade shared the details of the previous call with his supervisor over a horrible cup of coffee at the Pancake King. The Supervisory Special Agent was surprisingly easygoing and upbeat. He was bordering on giddy. He seemed to be more concerned with having a smooth press conference than hearing any of the details about the killer, the message Ming may have been trying to send, or the purpose of the whole deadly ordeal.

The statements for the press conference had already been written. The conference was scheduled for the late evening. Agency leaders figured many news outfits would be forced to "go live" to the conference, which was always more exciting for viewers.

The write up was pushed across the table for Cade's review, but not necessarily his approval. It was done in the same fashion as the car salesperson who thinks it's better to write down a price rather than say it out loud. Cade was frustrated to read the details of the case as described. Management seemed to know very little about the case. He decided to skip the press event if at all possible.

Cade's manager relayed the press event details and acted as though he actually thought Cade would be excited. After missing the mark with the press conference description, the boss handed over a "to do" list including photographing all crime scenes and the burned house. Cade was also ordered to interview Mrs. Ming immediately. It was obvious to Cade that Mrs. Ming had to be interviewed, but he resented being told to do it as if it wouldn't have occurred to him. It was also infuriating to him that everyone around him saw the fire and dead Mr. Ming as a major milestone, if not even a conclusion.

Cade left his boss who headed back to do whatever bosses do all day. Any resentment he may have had was tempered by the appreciation of being left alone to do his job. He headed straight to the Ming house without the slightest thought of how to conduct the most important interview he'd carried out in years. As he climbed the front steps, he decided to wing it, based on Mrs. Ming's level of participation. He was actually a little surprised that she answered the door.

The seasoned interviewer spent nearly two hours with Mrs. Ming who knew surprisingly very little about her husband's affairs. Ming spoke English fairly well, but Cade struggled to keep up at times. He followed along well enough to summarize her statement.

Mrs. Ming poured hot tea without asking Cade if he wanted any. He accepted it out of respect and choked down the bitter taste. Mrs. Ming used code words to describe her marriage. She said her husband was extremely dedicated to his job and research. Cade took this to mean he was never around. Ming said her husband's long hours and dedication to whatever he was working on caused him great stress and he was difficult at times. Cade knew he was an abusive husband.

Cade connected with the interviewee for some reason. At nearly the two hour mark, after a second cup of hot tea which tasted better than the first, Cade became a bit more direct. He moved his hand to Mrs. Ming's as a sign of support and because physical contact usually jumpstarts an interviewee for some reason. She sat in silence, continuing to stare out the window into the bright blue sky.

"Ma'am, we've gotta put this thing to rest. Have you heard about the case involving all the young men dying?"

"Yes," Ming responded, with a look on her face that asked what that had to do with her husband, the scientist.

"The same drugs that killed those boys were found in the house where your husband died. I think he was producing those drugs." Cade could see the news was a shock to the deceased's wife. "What was your husband working on? What was he involved in?" Ming looked back at Cade with swollen eyes.

"Agent Cade, regretfully, I don't know much about his working. Perhaps I know very little of this man after all. He was researching something he thought would make him rich, or famous. His obsession destroy our family and took away his daughters. He work all hours of the nights and could never be disturb. I cannot tell you that I am sad he is gone." It was one of the most powerful statements Cade had ever heard during an interview.

Ming left the dining room table and began to hand-wash their cups, ignoring the dishwasher by her side. "I think his research was for the government." The statement threw Cade for a loop because he had already formed the opinion that Ming was stable, even after losing her husband.

"What gives you that impression?" Cade asked, trying to sound as though he actually believed her. Ming stared out the small kitchen window as she spoke.

"Someone was visiting him very late at night. He drive a large black car. A very official and expensive car. It drive around to the back of the house. I never get too close. God only knows what he would have done if he'd seen me spy on him. I always think his work was for someone powerful and secret."

Cade felt the gravity of Mrs. Ming's words but paused to consider if the phrases "get too close" and "drive around," were intended to mean the car continued to visit. He decided after only a few seconds that, although Mrs. Ming had decent control of the English language, she was tripped up by past and present tense verbs.

Cade hit a mental speed bump. It is a common issue in interviewing, when the interview thinks things are going one way, and they suddenly take a turn. He was now at the cusp of getting case changing information as it was clear that others, and maybe others in more of a leadership role, were involved and on the run. He couldn't help thinking about of a bunch of overzealous media hounds getting ready for a bogus announcement.

"When is the last time you saw the sedan? Did you ever see anyone? Did your husband ever mention working with anyone at all?" Cade asked all three questions and had at least three more, but he stopped to allow her to catch up.

"My husband never discussed work. Never. And he never mention the cars, and I never saw anyone at all."

"Cars?" Cade asked with emphasis on the s, wondering if this was simply a misplaced letter and not meant to be plural.

"Yes. After the sedan stopped, maybe four week ago, a smaller, regular car came in its place." Cade dropped his head and raised his eyebrows before realizing his change in posture. He tried to shake it off and act as though this was not earth-shattering news but he could not stop from forming an expression of surprise. Ming caught the look on his face.

"I'm sorry, Agent, if this is important to your

investigation. I guess the big car that looked so official give me comfort that Chan was not involved in anything less than honorable." Cade thought about the word *honorable* and how it was so frequently used in the Asian culture. Maybe it was just those old karate movies.

"And I would request, please, that no police cars come back. Neighbors will know soon enough our trouble."

"Police cars?"

"Yesterday morning. A car was here after the news of the fire. I assure you there are no clues here to find."

Cade was furious but tried to conceal his frustration. The local police had avoided the case like the plague for the most part but now surfaced the day Mr. Ming was identified. The interview continued for another solid hour but with nothing more was gained. Cade learned nothing about the cars, the markings, not even the color. He knew Mrs. Ming had given all she could at least thirty minutes prior, but he didn't want to leave the woman for fear he'd forgotten to ask something that she knew but didn't find important. He gave out his second business card in two days. It was two more than he'd distributed in a nearly a year.

Cade picked up his cell phone to call his boss, but decided to call someone who'd be more helpful instead.

"Hey, Mad," Lester said in a rushed voice.

"I just left Mrs. Ming, and you're not gonna believe this can of worms."

"Hold on," Lester said. The muffled sound of kids in

the background told Cade that Lester was off duty. "Sorry, man," Lester said as he returned to the conversation. "Since I, I mean *we*, solved the big case, I took a few hours of leave. We've been at the pool for a little bit, and now I'm takin' 'em to dinner. I figured I'd use some of my time off now and avoid all the embarrassment of you giving me a big cash award at the press conference. I hear it's scheduled for this evening. You ironing your tie?" It was a bit of a cheap shot, Cade thought, because Lester knew he didn't have any interest in face time. He chalked it up to Lester being stressed over the family outing.

"Nobody is going to be doing any press conferences unless it's the Internal Affairs mopes," Cade said in a tension-building statement of his own.

"What?" Lester shot back, now with a changed tone and inflection in his voice. The background noise had faded, and Cade knew Lester had walked away from his family. He'd done it a hundred times himself.

"I need to see you in person to hash this out," Cade said, looking to reunite with his old partner.

"Listen, man, give me a couple of hours. The kids and wife will be happy, and maybe I'll get lucky later. The kids are driving me nuts already, and we haven't even left the driveway. I'll be back before CNN picks up the story, and we'll hit Margarita Grill. So what's this about I-A?"

"Those idiots are about to pull off a press conference, and we've got other players out there! Ming says a dark sedan was showing up to meet with her husband, the toasted chef. She called the car official and expensive. That kind of freaks me out, man."

"Could she I-D the driver if we take over some photos of all the dead players?" Lester asked as if he may risk divorce by cancelling dinner to help his running buddy. "Maybe it was the other marshmallow."

"She says she never saw anyone. I don't think they got out of the car. Maybe they just delivered or picked up something. Maybe it was the dope. I think she'll give us consent to search if I ask. I was waiting to get a team together."

"Listen, for all she knows, he may have been hookin' up with his old high school girlfriend in the driveway. You don't even know the cars are connected. He sounds like a creepy guy anyway. God knows what he was up to." Returning now to the wife and kids who were already inside the car, Lester said, "If she seemed cooperative, let's hold off and see what shakes out. Just give me a few hours, man. Even if there is someone else, your cooker is out of the picture."

For the first time since learning Ming was dead, Cade's sense of urgency returned. He wrapped his brain around the idea that there could have been previous batches of the poison made and available for delivery.

He let Lester get on his way even though he wanted to talk things out with somebody he trusted. Cade closed his phone then reopened it and reluctantly dialed his boss.

CHAPTER 21

Cade's supervisor jumped into supervisory mode and quickly dismissed Cade so he could begin a calling spree to modify the details presented at the press conference. The turn of events would certainly get him and a few other agency leaders on the evening news.

Within an hour, and not surprising to Cade, without many actual details, several media coordinators from three different agencies had outlined the details for a late evening news conference. The bureaucrats planned to describe, in terms more vague than the media wanted, events leading up to the fire which took the life of manufacturer of the doctored drugs. The man, who had earned a PhD in chemistry, had apparently used his impressive skill set for a sick killing spree.

The speaker or speakers would avoid saying the case was closed and would, instead, gingerly ask for any information about possible co-conspirators. Cade headed away from the city, down Highway 78, in a move that was intended to postpone his arrival back downtown. He would show up at the press event sloppily dressed and in no condition to be on camera or even acknowledged by management.

With a *ding* of alert regarding low fuel, Cade decided to test the fuel indicator and drive all the way to the Kangaroo Mart near Uncle Frank's. It was the last known location of Esposito before being taken into custody.

Cade secured the nozzle to run automatically and turned toward the big yellow Kangaroo. He wasn't sure that he cared, and certainly wasn't defending Esposito at this point, but he found it important to hear from the gas station manager why he had it in for Esposito.

Cade thought he was over his attempt to rehabilitate Esposito. Hearing what really happened on the day the trespasser was picked up may help solidify his desire to break free from his old friend once and for all.

"Yeah, I know Angelo. My daughter gave him that little dog," the owner said in a surprising show of disinterest.

"So what'd he do that made you call the police?" Cade asked.

"I didn't call the police. They saw him and picked him up. Must have had warrants or something." Cade could only mumble a "yeah." Once again, he found himself a bit puzzled regarding Esposito's actions.

Cade returned to the running pump and stood with one hand on the nozzle as the pump's cost display rapidly increased. He wanted to call Lester again to quiz him about going out of his way to arrest Esposito. He decided that, while a bit underhanded, Lester had been right about Esposito all along. Lester had much more experience with drug users, and he knew that change would be hard for Esposito. It might even be impossible for a man who lived so comfortably in the pit.

Cade purposely arrived fifteen minutes past the scheduled press event start time. The main conference room at the federal courthouse was arranged for the briefing, but the scattered agents and lack of press crew indicated a cancellation for some reason that didn't really concern Cade one way or another.

He was pleasantly surprised to see Officer Whitley, and the two made eye contact. Whitley headed through the crowd and out a side exit. She paused at the door to ensure Cade saw her and caught the invitation. Turning to leave from another exit, he was grabbed from behind by an agency executive. The man was so many levels above Cade in the food chain, Cade didn't even know who the man was. He hoped Whitley would wait for him.

The manager shook Cade's hand while grabbing his shoulder with his free hand. It was a move straight from the Bill Clinton book on how to shake hands and make someone feel you know them. Cade learned that the three agencies involved could not agree on how the announcement should be carried out. Even more of a problem was that they could not agree how to assign credit for solving the case. The press announcement had been postponed until Monday.

Actually, that's what he *heard*. What was actually told

to him was that the conference was postponed to allow him a few days to gather valuable information that would help in delivering a more thorough message to the public.

After his best performance on why he felt the government execs were the smartest people alive, Cade let the supervisor return to his handshaking and baby kissing. He reached the empty corridor with much disappointment. A strange whistle grabbed his attention, and he caught a glimpse of Whitley rounding a corner. He felt something very inappropriate was about to happen but he could not stop himself from following like a school boy knowing he was about to get into trouble.

Whitley had a look on her face like she absolutely could not get caught with Cade. And although he had prided himself in maintaining their friendship and never crossing the line, Cade could not help but like the sudden interest and strange behavior exhibited by Whitley.

Whitley began talking, but her words were so far from what Cade expected to hear, he struggled to catch up.

"I saw Esposito's bicycle in Warren's garage yesterday morning." Cade had been calling Warren by his last name for so long, he didn't realize, at first that Whitley was talking about Warren Lester. He repeated words of significance the way a trainer waves ammonia under the nose of a dazed athlete to bring him around. *Esposito, Warren, fire, bicycle.* Cade had at least twenty questions for Whitley, but for some reason he started with one not directly related to the case or the fire.

"What were you doing at Lester's?"

Whitley went on to briefly, and without detail, explain that she had been romantically involved with Lester for over a year. They met a couple times a week at Lester's home after Lester's wife headed off to work.

"We'll talk about that later, but I'm worried about Warren. He hates the city so much for putting him back on the streets. He wants to be a detective more than anything in the world. I think he's trying to screw with the investigators until he can solve the case on his own. He thinks he'll get invited back to the Detective's Division."

"He requested the move to spend more time with his wife." Cade said, not so much as a defender of Lester's actions but to remind Whitley that her apparent boyfriend was married.

"No, he was forced to step down, Maddy, because we got caught. It's not as bad as you think, but we did cross the line. " He stayed in the precinct to spend more time with me." Whitley put emphasis on the word *me* as she grabbed Cade's hand in a show of continued friendship. "Nobody pays attention when two cops meet at the courthouse or a county parking lot."

He aggressively pulled away from Whitley's touch and turned his back to her. Partly because he needed to decipher what, if anything, this had to do with his mess of a case. But he also felt a tinge of jealousy and hated her just for the moment.

Cade walked at lightning speed to the courthouse lobby and reviewed the log that all law enforcement officers were required to sign. Lester had not made an appearance. He hit the number two button of his speed dial to find out if Lester had made it back from his family outing. After a second thought, he closed his phone before pressing send.

He made it to the North Prescient in less time than it used to take him to make lunch dates with Lester. He badged the receptionist and motioned toward the Detective's Division. He never slowed, and the alert clerk pressed the door release button just as he grabbed the knob.

"Lester around?" he asked. The switchboard operator looked over her shoulder at another officer for an answer. The officer paused in her search for a case file.

"He's officially off today, but I think I saw him earlier. If his car's in the lot, he's probably in the squad room finishing reports, or he could be the locker room." Just as he typically failed to say goodbye, he left the radio room without a word of appreciation. He wandered through two aisles of naked men. He even stood a moment to look in the community shower at another half dozen nude cops. A couple of officers, either beginning their shifts or on their way home voiced their displeasure with Cade being in their space.

He walked through the locker room, out through the bathroom, and through the publicly accessible foyer leading outside. Finally, he spotted and locked in on

Lester who was transferring bags and personal belongings from the trunk of his squad car to his personal car parked in the adjacent space.

"Hey, hero. What did I miss?" Lester said, sounding confrontational, not sarcastic. He stood closer to Lester than necessary. He decided he should more carefully think about his opening argument when confronting someone in the future. Cade had to resolve the bicycle issue, but found it hard to speak. He wanted answers related to the burned grey goose and Officer Whitley.

"What do you want, Maddy?" Lester said, now with a touch of bitterness. Lester slammed his trunk in a show of force and power. The sound and changed attitude shocked Cade who stood flat on his feet. He squinted as the sun reflected directly into his eyes from the polished trunk of Lester's patrol car. The bright white paint had been recently washed and buffed, most likely by some city prisoner.

Cade felt a lump in his throat that made him feel like he could vomit. He could not stop his eyes from covering over with glossy pre-tear build up. The sight confused Lester who now stood with his developed chest inflated and his hands clinched in a show of an immediate altercation.

Cade, a bit shorter and lighter than Lester, looked directly into eyes of his friend. With a quick twist of his body, Cade firmly landed his right fist deep and directly into Lester's solar plexus. The surprising force of the blow sent Lester against his car, gasping for air.

Onlookers rushed to Lester's aid. Cade, the outsider to the off duty police officers, was forcefully tackled onto the unforgiving concrete. It took a full minute for Lester to regain his ability to breathe. He stood slowly and walked towards Cade who was still in the grip of the witnesses.

Cade's mind raced through images as he stood in confinement, anticipating certain pain. He stood as a defiant prisoner, seeing first the image of Mrs. Ming, her face filled with sadness but also with hope for a life without an abusive husband. He pictured the friendly smile of Esposito and could now easily see beyond the sores and aged lines on his face. He saw the face of a father, trying with all his might to protect a child who could not be protected from a disease.

And finally, Cade pictured the little boy under the steps, covered in sand and content to crash his model cars into each other for hours on end.

"Two-two-two-two," he must have been saying.

Lester moved away from his car with teeth and fists clinched. He walked away exposing the large blue number 22 painted on the trunk of his patrol car. The number designated his new patrol car. The marked unit had been assigned after Lester lost his dark unmarked sedan because of his poor choices involving Officer Whitley.

CHAPTER 22

The unmarked cars of the Alabama Bureau of Investigation made a horrific sound as they poured into the parking lot. All heads turned. Lester and Cade were the only two present who knew the purpose of yet another, even more surreal interruption.

Three men jumped from the cars holding their badges in the air, much like the federal agents are portrayed in the movies when they arrive on the scene at the last minute to take over the show. The state cars formed a barricade as a safety measure in case Lester would not come peacefully. Several of the ABI Agents stood behind the protection of their opened doors, with guns drawn and badges held high.

Between the black and blue of metal and uniform, both Cade and Lester could see the curly blonde hair of Tina Whitley. Cade instantly knew she had called in the Calvary after putting two and two together.

Lester was taken to a state holding facility where he was interviewed by everyone remotely involved in the

Doctor LNU case except for Maddison Cade, who refused. Lester would spend a full week locked up without speaking a word. Cade spent a week on administrative leave, trying to straighten his head, his heart and the volumes of paperwork that were required for his actions.

Just as Cade had envisioned, another press event was planned. Government leaders announced the tremendous effort by the federal government, assisted by several members of the Birmingham Police Department's Internal Affairs Division, and a confidential informant named Diez (Code named for his old jersey number).

They announced the imprisonment of one of the city's own for what they called "actions of obstruction to the investigation." One agency director assured the city the deaths were over and vowed to return to the podium a third time with a full briefing following full judicial action which was guaranteed to be severe and swift.

The press conference speakers were careful to dance around the unknown details of the case, which sadly included *all* the details. It wasn't the job of the executives to dig for answers, and Cade was simply not willing. The event brought numerous questions and just as many negative comments about all the agencies involved, so event planners kept it as short as possible.

With every law enforcer stationed within five miles attending the press conference, Cade escaped to the quietness of the regional office inside the federal building. He tried to envision what life would be like working in an office and not alone in his SUV all day. He imagined long lunches and laughter. When the front door buzzer startled him, he resented the intrusion.

It was an enormously ironic event that was missed by all involved. At the stroke of noon, following the lack-luster press event, exactly three months after the case was opened, a FedEx driver walked into the federal building. He held open the large glass door for several well-dressed government agents and managers who walked in the opposite direction, headed for a celebratory lunch. They had just completed telling all who would listen about their *solved* case.

Cade accepted the envelope from the man in purple and orange and did his best forgery of Veida's name on that tricky little glass signature pad. As he tossed the envelope on the mail desk, he was surprised to see his name in the addressee field.

He opened the plastic envelope to find another within. The plain white envelope had no return address. Typed in the middle of the envelope was the formal address of Cade's agency headquarters in Washington, DC. The address had been typed, marked through with a single black line, and "SA Cade – Southeast Division" had been written as a new destination. Somehow, he recognized the gravity of the message before it was read.

*Agent Cade, I hope this letter find you well. In straightening out financial and other matters left by my late husband...*Cade paused to consider if the choice of words was appropriate. He pictured the mound of dirt still on Ming's grave. *I learned of a safe deposit box. I only today removed the sparse contents of the box including this letter which I believe would be of more value to you.*

Cade felt a bit uncomfortable, thinking he was about to read what was surely going to be the very personal thoughts of a dead man. It was much like the way he felt during the execution of a search warrant, when he and other agents read personal notes and letters of crime suspects once they were removed from the scene in handcuffs.

My dearest Lili, I write to you with great sadness in my heart. My actions surely have caused you much pain and suffering. I will take shame to my grave. My greatest failure involves our most precious daughter. Please tell her every day I love her. I know my actions and short temper will forever haunt her memory. Several months ago, someone close to us reported seeing me strike her. I pray her forgiveness and confess this act to you. I was questioned by a police officer who failed to obtain the evidence he needed to pursue me legally. This past summer, having learned of my chemistry work at BSC, the officer returned to me with a threat to remove our Lin from our home if I did not help him. This officer assured me the chemicals I produced for him were not being used to harm. But as the weeks progressed, I feared just the opposite was being carried out. I do not know the details of this man's plan, but I believe I have been supporting an evil vendetta that has consumed him. Please forgive me. I beg you to restore our daughter's faith in love and family.

Cade read the letter twice to ensure he didn't miss a detail. He quickly logged on to the guest terminal of the Division's database and completed the closing Summary Report by referencing the letter. The file, the letter and the Closing Report were stapled together and placed in Cade's supervisor's inbox along with a dozen other case reports for review. He knew he was not handling the letter with the appropriate amount of attention, and he knew his supervisor would hit the roof in two days when he read it. He believed his resentment would be understood by all those above him in the agency hierarchy. They could plan a fourth press conference for all he cared.

CHAPTER 23

Two weeks had passed since the press briefing. The clock on his bedside table clicked past 7 a.m. and Cade rolled over, still asleep. He had become accustomed to sleeping late. He rarely got out of bed before seven. More importantly, he was ending his days earlier to catch up on time missed with Kelly and the kids.

He thought of Esposito nearly daily, but with new cases in the opposite direction of the city, and because Esposito had avoided incarceration, there was little need to make the drive. The two spoke daily, mostly about nothing of great importance; the same thing both men imagined friends talked about.

Some days, if deep in the middle of a report or case concentration, Cade avoided the phone when seeing Esposito's number on the Caller ID display. Many calls were turning into gripe sessions about how hard it is for felons or ex-drug users to get a decent job. Cade hated to let the friendship slip, but at times it was good to have one less stressor in his life. Rumors of Esposito's drug addiction and arrests continued to surface from time to time. Cade usually dismissed them with only brief consideration as to their accuracy.

Cade's phone buzzed off the night stand. He had not received such an early morning call since the Dr. LNU case closed weeks prior. He hung from the bed and recovered the phone. With one eye, he scrolled to the missed calls and saw the number of Esposito's mother's house. He thought briefly about how much red tape it would take to change his cell phone number.

He left the phone at his side and rolled over to wrap an arm around Kelly. Within thirty seconds or so, the phone chirped, indicating a voicemail had been left. He turned the phone off without opening his eyes. He would wait until well after his morning latte to listen to the latest excuse for some act Esposito really didn't commit.

After his feet hit the floor, just after eight, he forgot about the waiting message. By ten o'clock, he was well into mandatory paperwork when a second call came in from the Esposito home. Cade reluctantly answered and was not totally surprised that the caller was Teresa Esposito, not her son. He listened with a hand rubbing both temples. He agreed to meet Mrs. Esposito in Forestdale after lunch.

Cade entered the building through the glass doors. He was not surprised that he was one of only three men in the place wearing a tie. He quickly spotted Esposito and made his way to see his old friend. For a moment, he forgot his frustration over his friend's actions. For the first time in weeks, he sincerely hoped to have some closure on all the negative feelings. Cade wanted to hug him, but it wasn't allowed.

"You look good, man. You finally cleaned up. I ignored a few phone calls and this happened? You blaming me?" Esposito didn't speak, but the look on his face was one of contentment. He looked good. Maybe it was the new clothes. Maybe the haircut. "What have I done?" Cade asked himself in a whisper.

"Thanks for coming," said a faint voice. Cade wiped the tears before turning to face her. He pictured the conversation he'd had with her a month or so prior, when he said her son would end up dead or in jail. He had regretted saying it, but now the prediction had come to fruition with painful accuracy.

"He loved you like a brother. You were the only one who came back to him. Everybody else gave up. He's been dead to them for over twenty years, Maddy."

"I gave up on him," Cade said crying now without reserve.

"Don't ever think you took his life. He chose his own path, and you just made it easier for him to leave this world so full of people not willing to give second chances."

Cade left before the coffin was closed. He swore to visit the grave soon. He clung to the words that maybe Esposito was headed for this fate anyway, and his work and effort may have helped a little in the final days.

Cade closed his eyes and waited for some sort of a sign from Esposito.

"Oh come on, you freakin' jerk!"

"What? You love it, right?"

"You had to kill me? And your house isn't five thousand square feet. You got size issues, man." Esposito was trying to act mad but it was obvious he was impressed with Cade's writing skills. Cade laughed at his friend whom he had just killed in his first attempt at a new book.

"Look man, you want to sell a book or two. People don't really want happy endings, they want surprises. You need to die. Take one for the team. Most of the other stuff is true."

"What team? The team leader only buys me Taco Bell every few days," Esposito said with pretend hostility. Silence filled the car as Esposito ran his hand over the glossy cover of the book. It was ironic how he could clearly see his reflection over the title of the book printed in bold orange letters. First attempts at the book cover had a bright white pile of cocaine as an attention-grabber. The image had been replaced at the last minute.

Esposito studied the new image for a few seconds, trying to decide if it was his profile from days long gone, and if the darker profile was that of Cade's, representing his support from the shadows. He finally concluded that the profile represented most everybody, and the dark mirror image represented that part we all keep tucked away from others.

The cross on the book's cover and spine, which would be missed by most readers, had been Esposito's idea. It was his way of saying God shows up in everyone's life in small, sometimes unnoticed ways, patiently waiting to take control. It was a very simple proposition that Cade struggled to see because of the million dollar church buildings, high paid preachers and overall "business" that religion had become.

Esposito, the now ex-drug user, clean and sober for seven months and eleven days, credited God every day for his continued success. He felt no need to judge other's level of sincerity, and dealt directly with the *God of his understanding,* as he called Him during his N/A meetings. Esposito vowed to himself that he wouldn't give up on Cade's rehabilitation. His reflection appeared again.

"Man, I look like crap."

"Yeah, you do," Cade said, with a punch to the arm.

"I love you, brother."

"You too, you freakin' stunad."

Cade sat in the driveway alone for a few minutes, watching Esposito and Skip walk into their new home. It wasn't much bigger than Uncle Frank's, but it was in a better part of the city, and you couldn't see through the walls. Skip, the Heinz 57 breed, turned out to be a good-sized dog. A little skinny like his owner, but much healthier looking overall.

Esposito's only real worry these days would be waking up in time to make it to his ten dollar an hour roofing job. Cade knew he probably couldn't do the work

Esposito did every day, and the thought made him even more proud of his friend. He laughed at the sight of the old police auctioned Mercury under the carport. It still had the dents from Catfish's work boots. Cade's mind took him to places from junior high to the fabricated burial of his friend on his way home. His *new* home.

He pulled into the single-car garage of the apartment he'd called home for nearly six months now since the separation from Kelly. It wasn't as spacious as the three-car garage. Kelly's car and the kids' bicycles filled that one now. Boxes were packed and his sparse belongings were ready to move again. The near-vacant apartment was a good analogy of his life without Kelly and the kids. Her ultimatum six months ago had been a wakeup call for Cade, and he struggled every day to be the kind of husband and father his family needed.

Frequent calls from Esposito, his counselor, helped him stay focused on the important things in life. Esposito continued to share signs of miracles in his life, direct touches from God, but Cade, ever the cynic, was slow to evolve.

During his six month recovery process, he had given up on Oprah, and even the lesser-known local goofball radio personalities. Instead, with permission from his Internal Affairs of course, he launched a part-time passion of public speaking. He also gave up the high-priced speaking gigs he had conjured in his head. They were replaced with smaller audiences of mostly acne-faced teens, eager to hear stories, whether real or fabricated.

Although Cade still enjoyed the occasional fantasy about fat royalties and book signings, their journey brought Cade and Esposito together in a way they never expected. Even though Cade tried to inspire Esposito to change, he learned that change would come only when Esposito was ready. And for his part, Esposito learned that Cade's addictions were easier to ignore, but just as deadly. Neither gave up on the other's rehabilitation.

With disaster quickly approaching, Cade realized that his interests and motivation in life had robbed him of precious time and experiences he will never see again.

Because Esposito had seen rock bottom, he was able to appreciate the value of true friendship. He knew how to soak up a few minutes of meaningless television with an uncle who may not live much longer. He even appreciated the unconditional loyalty and companionship given by a dog. With Esposito as a coach, Cade was finally coming to realize that success is not just checking off a goal. He learned that to determine true success in life, one must first measure the value of the goal, whether reached or not.

Far too many karate lessons, piano recitals and birthday parties had been missed because of Cade's misconception of success. With Esposito's help, Cade would overcome his issues and rebuild a life of true happiness with his wife and his children. In the six months Cade lived by himself, the quiet reflection did wonders for his recovery.

Kelly was the first to recognize the change in Cade and she happily accepted him back into their estate home. Their first decision after reuniting was to sell the home for a smaller three bedroom inside a quaint, less prestigious community. Cade made it home for most dinners and plenty of evening family time. He quickly learned that he could spend less time on the job but accomplish more overall because his new home life energized him daily.

CHAPTER 24

Two days after Christmas, the final manuscript was submitted to the one literary agent who agreed to review their work. As is typical for new authors, the manuscript was passed around for months before a decision was rendered. When the agency's decision came by e-mail, Cade stared at the computer screen for over three minutes, mumbling to himself in disbelief. He read the phrases, "representing you," and "as your agent," at least a dozen different times with varying inflection in his voice.

The follow up phone call from the young New York editor set a more serious tone. With a strong Boston accent, the editor/agent warned of the pending effort needed to make the book "marketable." He used as an example that Cade had focused on the book's lead character and failed to "bring to life" those around him including his wife and kids. Cade didn't know if the editor credited the book's shortcomings with the inexperience of its writer, or if he suspected that the book's lead character and its author shared the same defects.

During the painfully long editing process that lasted six months into the new year, Cade and Esposito lost count of the church and school groups they visited. There were more offers than the two, both trying to keep a "day job" alive, could juggle. Esposito turned down countless "love offerings," and donations, and kept Cade, still fighting his desire for the tangible, from accepting any fees for his "performances."

Over at least thirty-five more Taco Bell trips, the rehabilitation continued. Esposito helped make a more "marketable" man out of Cade during the days, while New York literary agents did the same to Cade's novel during long evening and weekend editing sessions. Esposito seemed to be trying to save Cade in spite of his own frustrations in the world that existed because of a past that would not go away.

CHAPTER 25

On July 1st, a modest offer was received from a New York publisher. Cade did not immediately share the news with his co-author, but instead, loaded the family into their new minivan and headed to the beach for a private celebration.

Cade and Kelly had purchased the "gently used" van to save money that could be spent on more important things like family getaways. It was another sign of Cade's successful rehabilitation. Cade decided he would wait to bring Esposito in on the celebration after all the details of the publisher's offer were nailed down.

After just three days at the beach, the family packed to return home for ribs and fireworks with the extended family. Cade, who was becoming accustomed now to putting his family before his cell phone, actually packed the phone in his luggage for the five hour drive. Nearly halfway home, during a leg stretching stop, Cade heard the familiar chirp, alerting him to a new voicemail message. He turned off the phone and put it out of his mind for a couple more uninterrupted hours with his family.

After both kids were bathed and fed, Cade retrieved the phone to check his messages. He sat on the swing of the front porch out of sight. He hoped that one day the image of him constantly talking on his cell phone would fade from his kids' memories. He watched Kelly moving around the family room with the kids, all three laughing. He thought again just how lucky he was.

He looked away from his family only after recognizing the concern in the familiar voice.

"Maddy, this is Tess Esposito. It's the 4th. Not sure if you're in town. Angi's gone. He left you a note. I'll be here all day tomorrow."

Cade missed a night of sleep. Luckily, his prior work schedule had trained him well for this. Now that he was back in Kelly's bed, he hated to leave so early. But even she realized the significance of the day. She got up with her husband to help get him on his way.

The television in the Esposito home was blaring but no one was watching. Mrs. Esposito was sitting at the kitchen table with a coffee cup Cade recognized as coming from the Kangaroo Gas Station by Uncle Frank's house. Cade walked down the short hallway, lined with freshly painted drywall. It was most likely a contribution from Esposito after he landed the last job.

"Coffee?" she offered, but Cade knew there was no coffee other than the cup she had brought, and she probably had no idea what she was saying. She slid the typed note across the wobbly kitchen table.

"He typed it on his new computer, and he left you the computer, too. It's in my car."

Sorry Maddy. Sorry for all the wasted time and energy. You never gave up on me and I made it. I'm like Jordan, going out on top. I can't imagine doing any better than I am right now. Thanks for your friendship. If we ever make a dime on the book, use it to take care of Skip. Independence Day. How ironic. I love you, man.

EPILOGUE

Special Agent Maddison Cade is now a better investigator, better husband, better father and a better friend. He faced his career's most challenging case and his life's most challenging issues.

Along the way, he reunited with his old high school friend, who knew so much about life even though most of his had been consumed with drugs, theft and deception.

Cade found clues to solve the case of his career and both men got a little closer to true happiness. In the end, one man helped the other in a way no one had, and pulled him from his addictions to a better life.

This was a story about one recovering drug user and one addict.

THE INSPIRATION

Many "scenes" from the book, while fictional, were inspired by events I experienced on the streets of Birmingham, Alabama and Washington DC. My initial goal was to produce a stand-alone crime fiction novel following the basic premise of an investigator trying to solve a case, with readers following along, guessing and second guessing the outcome. Moreover, the goal was to speak to audiences of thousands and to sell a billion copies of this book and the books to follow. Two decades of criminal investigation aided in the scene creations, but completing the work without the final moral-to-the-story ending would have made The Addict, initially entitled *Magic City Murders*, just another crime fiction.

The inspiration for the book's modification came from individuals who surfaced (or re-surfaced) in my life near the final editing stage. After years of chasing "bad guys," I reunited with a few old friends who, for some reason, relayed parts of their dark past and their ongoing struggles to find success in life. Success for one included keeping a job while visiting probation officers twice weekly; for another, it was staying sober for one more hour; and for the third, it was finding a way to silence outside forces by finding the next fix. For the first time in my life, I saw the people behind the addiction. At the time, *addict* was just another word for *criminal*.

This book was not intended to highlight poor choices. After all, each man made a choice which started his downward spiral. Instead, it is in part a celebration of overcoming obstacles and finding *success*. More importantly, it's a challenge to re-evaluate the word success in our own lives, regardless of social status.

The book was not written as a religious tool either, however, it is a fact that two of the men who inspired this book made decisions to give what remained of their trampled lives to God. It turns out, there appears to be no waiting period and no lengthy application process when choosing this route. Forgetting for a moment how they reached their lowest points, but considering how they climbed from the darkest lows to their current outlook on life (this one and the next), I consider them extremely successful.

I sincerely hope this work is of some benefit beyond being an entertaining brief escape from reality. Personally, my experiences with these and others fighting an addiction of some sort, whether socially acceptable or otherwise, have led me to abandon the dreams of sold-out book tours in exchange for the possibility that the words herein have caused something positive in your life.

AKNOWLEDGEMENTS

Preston: I think about you every single day. Thanks for your service to our great state and the federal government. Thank you for your friendship. You are truly a hero. I will share some of what I learned from you with the young people who I am so fortunate to work with. I miss you, man.

Kel: To steal a line from Agent Cade, you are my best friend, soul mate and the calming force in our hectic life. Thank you for putting up with this and all the other crazy projects over the years. I love you.

Georgia Babee de Maximus: June 15, 2004 – July 22, 2010 Loyal protector and friend offering unconditional affection. You are missed.

So many friends have supported this project. I can't thank you enough: Dixie, Sue Hamlett, Lee Summerlin, Cyndi Calhoun, Charlie Summerlin, Allan & Annette Davis, Bob and Kathy Esper, Donna Tubbs, Lou Riddell, Matt Shores, (Sister Figure) Donna Logan, Bill Pugh, Jack Owens, Chuck Whitlock, Ann and Jay Price, Bill and Carol Walther, Tim Gangloff, Will Sorrell, Jackie Hester, Karen Nesmith Poe, Sammy Guarino, Parrish Spates, Kevin Grandy, Tina Parker, Laura Partain, Kathy Berg, Jeff Wingo, Anthony and Michelle Russo, Rick Jaffe, Randy Teeter, Sherri Spears, Cari Foulk, Jonathan Clements, Jay Pesek, Mr. and Mrs. Faught and the Madison Academy Mustangs, students of Bottenfield Jr. High School, Suzanne Monosky, Anna Maria Tucker, Rebecca Mannerly, the Ball family, Mike and Amy Brown, Rebecca Rutherford, Dr. David Dyson, Bob Moats, Jeremy Burrell, Selena Franklin Harper, the men and women of the Old Firehouse Shelter.

ABOUT THE AUTHOR

Bob Kuykendall began his federal government career in 1987, inside the mailroom of the FBI. He has since worked for three different federal agencies, chasing alleged fraudsters, bombers, child abusers and the garden-variety law breaker. Bob's investigative challenges have created a man who relates to life's journey in an unusual and perhaps unorthodox way, and this style has spilled over into his writing and speaking.

Following the September 2001 terrorist attack, in an effort to return closer to home, Bob accepted a Special Agent position with the FDA's Office of Criminal Investigations in Atlanta, Georgia. In 2005, Bob and his family returned *home* to Birmingham, Alabama to help form the Birmingham Domicile of the FDA's Office of Criminal Investigations. The move, both physical and psychological, would be the impetus for the Maddison Cade series including The Addict, Undercover, and others yet to make it from brain to book.

Bob's broad experiences in the government and on the street have led to national recognition as a public speaker in many areas including fraud reduction, security, interview and negotiation, goals and objectives, task management and effective communication strategies. During his tenure as a federal agent, Bob has spoken to groups ranging from a handful of senior citizens in the basement of a local church, to government leaders including White House and Congressional staff members.

Bob obtained his undergraduate degree from the University of Alabama at Birmingham and a Master's Degree in Economic Crime Management from Utica College of Syracuse University.

Bob, his wife Kelly, and his kids Madelyn and Cade reside in Birmingham.

Search & Seizure – of Opportunity for Effectiveness

The following is an excerpt from presentation material created by the author to help you reflect on your past decisions and perhaps decisions necessary for your successful life journey.

Now that you have learned the fate of (and weaknesses of) Special Agent Cade, I hope you may use the following for book reflection/discussion, and perhaps reflection of a more personal nature.

The I AM Theory

Years ago, I was taking a flight to a small town outside Houston, Texas. During one short and uncomfortable part of the trip, I found myself on an eight-passenger prop-plane making a "quick jump" to a small airport. I remember hearing the word "jump," and thinking it was not a word that should be used by a flight attendant in any conversation, ever. It's amazing how clearly you can concentrate about your life and deep philosophical matters immediately after boarding a plane and being asked your weight so they know how much fuel to load.

As we were bumping over air pockets and descending over small homes and trailers, I clearly saw one tiny home which sat all alone. It was in a large clearing with no other signs of human existence for miles. It was similar to other small homes we flew over, but this one had infant toys scattered across the yard. I mentally created a vision of a young couple which I figured decided, right after marriage, to get away to a remote place with no intrusions. Sure, they had to pack a lunch to go "into town" to get groceries, but the solitude and privacy was probably worth it.

I assumed that at some point, the solitude and privacy led to the birth of a new family member. I pictured these two young adults in my mind, probably nothing close to the actual couple. I wanted to ask if they ever re-thought their previous interests and home selection now that a child was growing up in this isolated home. I wondered if the solitude had become such a part of their lives, they didn't consider a new direction after the baby was born.

I developed a theory about decisions we make that bring us to where we end up in life. The concept works by you filling in the sentence, "I am (blank)." It could be personal: "I am struggling with an addiction." It could be very personal: "I am sad because I can't keep a girlfriend."

The I AM Theory is a suggestion of how you got to whatever state of being you used to fill in the blank.

Interests

We each have hundreds and maybe thousands of interests. Some are crazy, like the time I got the urge to go skydiving. Some are more sensible, like my interest in providing for my family. Sometimes interests compete, like my skydiving interest and my interest in not dying so I can be *not dead* while I take care of my family.

You may believe you have an interest like, "keeping a job," but if you think about it a moment, you may realize you don't enjoy working, but you do need the income. To take it one step further, you may not care about money or insurance, but your ultimate interest is to supply your basic needs like food and shelter, which of course, takes money.

Action

Every day, we take action based on which interests rise to the top of our list. The alarm goes off and you really have an interest in smashing it into a thousand pieces. But you need to keep that job, so you decide to get out of bed and be on time. You may also have an interest in seeing the new cute guy from the loading dock, so the two interests team up to help get you moving.

Our list may contain interests that just linger. How many times do you think, *That would be nice if I only had the time,* or, *If I would have done that while I had the chance,* etc? You never really ignore an interest; you just act on those with more pull.

At some point, we finally decide to do something about an interest. If I wanted to finally go skydiving, I would just look up the number and get directions. I would go to the airfield, pay a fee, sit through classroom instruction and a few exercises, then jump.

Immediately after taking an action, we experience a reaction. It may be good. It may be not so good. If, after five hours of skydiving preparation, I jumped and safely fell to earth, that would be action and a positive reaction. If I wet my pants in free fall, that would be a negative reaction. (For me and those already on the landing zone.) When the result of our action (the reaction) is negative, as in my graphic and gross skydiving scenario, the interest simply fades away to be replaced by another.

Motivation

If our action is met by a positive, pleasant or productive reaction, the interest remains and maybe even grows. We remain interested (motivated) to carry out this action again. Motivation brings repetition because our interest remains to be acted upon over and over. Through repetition, the interest becomes more a part of us and what we do.

In our lives, we tend to take action or do things the same way we did yesterday because it worked out well for us. Perhaps, sometimes this doesn't mean the action was great, or even positive, it just was good enough or maybe it simply wasn't bad.

Unfortunately, many who read this will be like the

estimated seven out of ten American adults who are not happy with their jobs. If you are a young person reading this, you now have an opportunity to avoid going down a path that is just "good enough." You are now making decisions that will affect your life for years to come. Please, enjoy your youth, but slow down and make the right choices. Do not settle for something that will not make you truly happy!

If you speak with people who confirm they are not where they wish they would have gone in life, it may be because at some point, they lost the motivation to act because the M in their I AM Theory changed from motivation to *momentum*. And many of us sometimes stay the course because it feels like momentum has carried us too far to return to a path of happiness.

Momentum

Activities are sometimes continued in our life and/or business because of a "good enough" type of thinking. We often settle for something that doesn't really motivate us any longer, but because the reaction isn't horrible, we may feel at least it's better than exerting energy to try something new. Also, doing the same thing usually means avoiding taking a chance that may result in failure. By doing the same old thing, we avoid failure, but we lose the opportunity of experiencing what could be.

Cade's actions to find success in the workplace should have been replaced, or at least modified over the years by actions to succeed in his own house as a good husband and a father.

Maddison Cade chased misplaced goals and became addicted to useless labels and recognition. Change was difficult.

If you are still one hundred or less (our life expectancy should be 120 years) you have plenty of time left. Take a leap of faith from your path to a new one that will more directly reach your goal. If you are younger, and you are just choosing your life's path, choose wisely and do not settle. Reach for the stars. You will do great things. Remember, you can always be addicted - *to life.*

FOR DISCUSSION:

What advice would you give to someone ten years younger than you?

What is the definition of the word success?

How does the word success relate to the word succeed?

Can you describe a situation where an individual may succeed but find no success?

Is it possible to be successful if you reach a goal that has no positive influence on family, friends or society?

Make a list now of ten goals you have set for yourself. Return to these goals in one year and determine if they are still of interest. You may find that some goals no longer exist, or have been modified.

Is it failure to give up on a goal?

What is the difference between failing to reach a goal and changing a goal?

What advice do you believe was written down to the first question by someone ten years older than you?

Made in the USA
Columbia, SC
26 May 2021

38544901R00159